Say What?

To the Willard Family...
with blessings!

Say What?

5 TALKS EVERY TEEN NEEDS TO HEAR

Derek A. Nicksich

Zion Press

Zion Press

CrossLink Publishing
1601 Mt. Rushmore Rd, STE 3288
Rapid City, SD 57702

Ordering Information:
Quantity sales. Special discounts are available on quantity purchases by corporations, associations, and others. For details, contact the "Special Sales Department" at the address above.

Say What?/Nicksich —1st ed.

ISBN 978-1-63357-314-7

Library of Congress Control Number: 2020934782

First edition: 10 9 8 7 6 5 4 3 2 1

PRAISE FOR *Say What?*

Derek Nicksich does an outstanding job of using humor (just self-deprecating enough) and wisdom to give teenagers advice for navigating the landmines of dating and sex, friendship, family relationships and finances. Never condescending, always empathetic and consistently wise in the contextual application of Scripture, this valuable resource succeeds in engaging the minds and spirits of teenagers searching for the heart of God. It should be required reading for teens and their leaders alike.

—**Jill Baughan,** Speaker & Author of *Born to Be Wild: Rediscover the Freedom of Fun* and *Hope Deferred: A Couple's Guide to Coping with Infertillty*

"If I could have read this book when I was a teen, it may have spared me from years of struggles. Through Biblical truth, engaging stories, and practical advice, Derek explores five crucial topics that often go unaddressed. Derek elevates the name of Jesus and calls a generation to follow Him in practical ways."

—**Ben Bennett**, Speaker & Author
Josh McDowell Ministry

This is a great book full of scripture and I, as a teenager, will say that this book has valuable lessons for all teenagers to learn. I recall many phone conversations where Derek, my youth pastor, walked me through the material in this book. It is a great teaching tool, and it has both helped me and taught me a lot.

—**Morgan Boschen**, 10th Grade Student
High School Trib3 Student Ministries,
Cool Spring Baptist Church

"I wish every teen would read this book. Derek is a student minister who very creatively speaks to kids about important issues in their life. This book is filled with fun stories, God-honoring insight, challenge, and intrigue. It's a compelling read. Derek is a great writer and communicator and he 'gets teens.'"

—**Jim Burns**, PhD & President, HomeWord
Author of *The Purity Code* and *Understanding Your Teen*

"As a mother of two teenagers and a young adult, this book is a valuable resource. While our culture increasingly rejects the Biblical worldview, Derek writes a practical guide that compels teenagers to follow God's word. He tackles important questions regarding dating, sex, and relationships with wisdom and the counsel of scripture. It's a book every Christian parent should read with their teenager!"

—**Julie Klose**, Blogger & Author
Giving Hope An Address: The Teen Challenge Legacy Story

"Derek's deep knowledge and love for teens shines through in this book with engaging stories that make his points memorable. It is impactful, concise, and easy to read; biblically-based and practical for today; challenging and relatable. This book, including discussion questions and action points, will be a blessing for teens and their parents who read it, discuss it, and apply its precepts."

—**Phillip M. Gerk**, PharmD, PhD
Father of three teenagers & Associate Professor (VCU)

"Having worked with teenagers for several years now, I am constantly looking for biblically-sound and relevant resources. Written with the teenager in mind, Say What? is undoubtedly a resource that meets this criteria. Derek incorporates wisdom, life experience, and humor to address real topics, such as dating and family matters, that teens deal with everyday. In a culture that seeks truth in a myriad of places, Derek wisely begins and ends with scripture, acknowledging that Christ is the ultimate source of truth."

—**David Moore**, Middle School Minister
Cool Spring Baptist Church

"I wish this book was around when I was raising teens! But then, my son is the author so I guess he learned a few things about these sensitive topics. As both a Minister and Writer (not merely as a Father) I recommend this book. Don't know where to start addressing tough topics? Here's five talks to strengthen your family and help prepare your teens for life."

—**Dan Nicksich**, Senior Minister,
Vanville Church of Christ

So often, Christian teens are told messages by the world that conflict with what God wants for their lives. Derek, my youth pastor, is a great writer and shares his advice in a non-judgmental, straightforward way indicating the serious impact of their decisions. His work gives teens like me a road map showing us how to serve Jesus in every area of our lives and inspiring us to do so.

—**Ryan Sherrill**, 10th Grade Student
High School Trib3 Student Ministries
Cool Spring Baptist Church

"In today's permissive culture both teens and their parents need help to hold on to their Christian values and resist the attacks of a godless culture. Derek's book provides that much needed assistance. Easy to read, engaging and on point, both parents and teens will be encouraged and emboldened to live more Christlike lives."

—**Bob Russell**, Retired Senior Minister
Southeast Christian Church
Author of *After Fifty Years of Ministry* and *When God Builds a Church*

"If you are going to say something to influence a teen today, it better be humorous, clear, and concise. Derek's five simple messages are like perfectly crafted Instagram posts: They make you look and then want to pass them on. From his sticky stories to his simple applications, these messages will point teens to God's will... and that is a point our world desperately needs to get!"

—**Jeff Walling**, Director, Youth Leadership Initiative
Pepperdine University
Author of *Daring to Dance with God* and *Until I Return*

DEDICATION

To High School TRIB3. You have brought much joy and humility into my life. I am grateful for your love, prayers, and encouragement. This book is dedicated to you. You are my flock, and I willingly shepherd you to follow our chief Shepherd, Jesus Christ.

"Shepherd the flock of God that is among you, exercising oversight, not under compulsion, but willingly, as God would have you; not for shameful gain; but eagerly; not domineering over those in your charge, but being examples to the flock. And when the chief Shepherd appears, you will receive the unfading crown of glory."

- 1 Peter 5:2-4 -

Contents

ACKNOWLEDGMENTS

Every book carries a toll with it. There is a transaction for time and labor with both writing and purchasing. No one experiences the weight of that transaction more than my lovely wife, Hannah. Thank you for supporting me in my calling.

Every book needs an editor. Daniel Francis Nicksich has proven generous and kind in that regard more than once for me. I am thankful for my dad, and his generosity toward my family and myself.

Every book should also have a second editor. To Jill Baughan, thank you for your encouragement, generosity, and keen editing mind. Here's to finding joy, no matter what.

Every book has a beginning, an origin story. This story started ten years ago with the man who drove me from Somerset, Pennsylvania to Knoxville, Tennessee in the spring of 2009. Visiting Johnson Bible College, his alma mater and now my own, would forever change my life. Thank you Brad for being my first and only youth pastor.

Each book has an army of support behind it. Thank you to CrossLink Publishing for their encouragement and work in making this project come to life.

FOREWORD

I learned a long time ago that lack of communication is to blame for many relational and life challenges. As a pastor, husband, dad, and friend, I've witnessed this too often in the lives of others and in my own life. Conversation is essential for healthy, functional lives and is what I love about Derek's book. The foundation of every chapter is about communication.

Parents struggle with timing and subject matter. How do you have a conversation about dating, sex, friendships, family, and money? On what resources do you rely? These are hot topics and are must-have conversations with students. Derek's format is easy to read, grounded in Scripture, and illustrated with stories. Every chapter ends with questions for reflection and dialogue.

In my experience, meaningful conversations come with questions. Authentic talks are two-way streets that allow us to listen and learn from each other. This book is a great tool to introduce the topic. Read it and ask the questions. Have meaningful discussions with those who matter most to you. You'll be glad you did. Derek, thank you for helping families tackle real-life issues.

—Brad Hoffmann
Pastor, Friend, Co-author of
Preventing Ministry Failure

INTRODUCTION

At the age of twenty-seven, almost ten years removed from high school, I was speaking to fifty high school students every Sunday and Wednesday. Often, I imagined myself like a fish flopping around gasping for air in between messages. I was struggling to breathe, think, and speak.

By the grace of God, I was surrounded by seventeen adults with an equal passion and calling to evangelize, disciple, and deploy students for the glory of God. My task of weekly preaching preparation, though daunting at times, is something God has equipped and called me to engage in. I rest in the power of timeless truth that applies to any person in any place at any time. That timeless truth is found in the laws of nature, the witness of creation, and in the revelation of God's character in the Scriptures. It is from the Bible that I teach every week.

The product of this book emerged from five talks I gave to the high school students at Cool Spring Baptist Church in Mechanicsville, VA. As I sought the appropriate subjects to preach about, the Spirit of truth led us into five weighty, difficult, and universally applicable subjects. Over the course of two months, we examined five questions pertinent to any teen at any time:

1. How should I approach dating?
2. How should I view sex?
3. What should I look for in a friend?
4. What is my role in the family?
5. How should I approach finances?

For each of these questions, we looked at how the Bible answered the question for us. It was amazing to see how the truth of Scripture is applicable to every generation in every culture at any time. I received great responses from students and adults alike respecting these talks. Though my heart found encouragement from their lips regarding my words, the real power in these talks rested in truth derived from God for His people.

Throughout these pages, you will find personal stories from my own teenage years, and from the present day as well. However, you will always find the Bible providing a resounding anchor. It was the apostle Paul, writing to his young protégé Timothy, who said, "All Scripture is breathed out by God and profitable for teaching, for reproof, for correction, and for training in righteousness, that the man of God may be complete, equipped for every good work" (2 Tim. 3:16-17).

Essentially, Paul reminds us that the Bible originates from God and is inspired by the Holy Spirit. Furthermore, he articulates four benefits any person, regardless of age, will gain from Holy Scripture. It is good for anyone who hears it, reads it, or memorizes it because it teaches us what we should know and should not know; should do and should not do. With that simple framework, the purpose of the Word of God is so that any man or woman, teenager or child, will find training for life.

God desires to train you for right living and right thinking through His training manual. This educational and experiential regimen is written with the intention of fulfilling the "good works which God prepared beforehand, that we should walk in them" (Eph. 2:10). There is much training that teenagers need today. There is much teaching regarding life that they are in desperate need of. This book contains five of those teachings, which carry devastating effects for teenagers today. My prayer for you, then, is that you would learn from the Word of God.

Every talk is given with the intention of placing what God has said before your very heart, mind, and soul. The stakes are high.

The opposition is fierce. Your flesh rages against the truth of God. The world beckons you away from the truth of God. Satan exists and distorts the truth of God.

I pray your ears would open to the truth. May you hear from the true Word of God. May you hear the truth from the incarnate Jesus Christ. May you hear how God desires you to approach dating. May you hear what God really thinks about sex. May you hear how important your friends are, and how to both be a good friend and find good friends. May you understand your God-given and God-defined role within the family. May you understand the weighty responsibility, as well as the dangers and snares, that finances present to every teenager.

To the teenager reading this book: I was in your shoes once. I wish I had read this book when I was a teenager. I wish I had sat through these talks, and actually remembered them. I wish I had applied what I heard, knew, and often rejected. This book is for me as much as it is for you.

To the small group leader, parent, or youth pastor reading this book: I was and am in your shoes. I lead seventeen small group leaders. I am a parent. I am a student minister. May you continue to spur your flock, children, or ministry on to love and good deeds (Hebrews 10:24) as I also strive to do in this brief book. I pray this resource will enable and encourage you to do that.

To the parent especially: Invite your teenager to read this book with you. Many teenagers do not pick up books and read them. Yet, if they are invited along on a journey, they are far more apt to listen, read, and discuss that which you draw out of them. My prayer is that you will draw out the deep desires and struggles of their soul and give them what they need to hear. This book is an endeavor to aid you in that holy pursuit.

DATING FAILS

Awkward dates. They have happened to many of us. The internet is filled with stories of tremendous failures in the area of courtship. I recently heard the story of one man's horrific, hilarious, and downright awkward first date.[1] For the sake of anonymity, we will name these fateful love birds Sandy and Danny.

Sitting in his college class, Danny noticed Sandy a few rows ahead of him. Initially, his eyes were not drawn to her figure but her computer screen. While Danny observed, Sandy sat through the professor's lecture researching golf clubs online. Seeing as Danny was a golfer himself, he was immediately intrigued. Hoping for a conversation starter between the two of them, Danny envisioned a future friendship blossoming with the possibility of romance on the horizon.

When the lecture concluded, Danny introduced himself to Sandy. Striking up a conversation, he segued to golf and sparks seemed to fly in the air. Their conversation led to phone numbers being exchanged, and eventually a golf date at the local country club was planned.

The golf outing arrived and the first few holes went well. That was, until the seventh hole began. Danny hit his drive and powered the ball onto the fairway. Sandy followed suit, but was slightly behind him. Being a gentleman, he allowed her to hit first. Then, lining up his shot, he determined a 3-wood was necessary for the two hundred and thirty yards displacing his ball from the fairway.

Before Danny made contact with the ball, he noticed a pair of sandhill cranes about one hundred and fifty yards down the fairway. Thinking they were not in harm's way, he proceeded to drive his shot. To his surprise, the ball stayed low, hovering over the ground like Luke Skywalker's land speeder in Star Wars: Episode IV. Picking up momentum, to both Danny and Sandy's horror, the ball streaked in a direct line toward the birds, striking one of the sandhill cranes in the neck, killing it instantly.

The story gets worse. Sandhill cranes mate for life. If either the male or female dies, the other bird will sit for hours crying over its lost mate. It was an emotional sight, like an episode of Law & Order: SCU (Sandhill Cranes Unit). A bird mourning its lost mate. If you thought that was bad, it got even worse. To Danny's surprise, Sandy loved sandhill cranes—in fact, they were her favorite birds. The look on her face was one of horror, disgust, and deep sadness. She broke down in tears. Danny and Sandy played the last two holes of golf in near silence. Concluding their game, they exchanged only a few words before the two fateful "love birds" said their goodbyes forever. Danny felt like taking a golf ball to his own neck after that date.

Dating is awkward at times. It is especially awkward for Christians. The reason dating is awkward is because God did not create "the date," culture did. What God did create is a desire within us to relate with others. God also created a desire within many of us to mate with one significant other, a husband or wife, of the opposite sex. The reason many Christians feel awkward about the subject of dating lies in the reality that the Scriptures remain silent about the matter.

If God created us with a propensity to relate with the purpose of finding a mate (Genesis 1:28), that leaves us with the question, "How should a Christian approach the date?" In other words, to reframe the question, if the Bible was written in various cultures and times where dating did not exist, how is a contemporary Christian teenager supposed to approach dating?

Teens today should do as other teens have done for centuries. Read the Bible. I know what you are thinking: "I thought you just said the Bible doesn't talk about dating?" It doesn't. However, it is sufficient to find the answers to any and every question you will ever have about life. Why do I think this? The Bible says so itself. 2 Timothy 3:16-17 says, "All Scripture is breathed out by God and profitable for teaching, for reproof, for correction, and for training in righteousness, that the man of God may be complete, equipped for every good work."

God has a good work for you to complete in life. This good work is bringing glory to Him by living wisely and seeking godliness in every area of life. With that said, you could say that God has a good work for you to complete in dating. It is this good work of dating that you need equipping for, and the training manual for the course is the Word of God.

The Scripture originates from God, as He spoke it into being. Since it is from God, who is infinitely wise, His Word is profitable and beneficial to all of us. His words, which are good because they come from a good God, teach us what is right in the world and what is wrong. They teach us how to *get* right with God and others, and how to *stay* right with God and others. This regimen of teaching, reproof, correction, and training even applies to the subject of dating.

The Bible tells us how to date right and how to date wrong. It tells us how to get our dating right and how to stay right within our dating. God desires for you to learn how to relate on a date so that you can find a mate. God does not desire for you to fail at dating. God does not desire for you to strike a sandhill crane with a fatal swing on your first date. It is never the Creator's fault when we make mistakes while dating. That guy made a mistake, and it cost him. It also cost the bird. God desires for you to succeed in dating, not to succeed in killing birds and your chances at marriage. In order to win, God gives us at least four principles to guide our swings. These four principles, straight from God and found within the Bible, will help us answer the question, "How should I approach dating?"

Prepare Practically

The first principle that should guide our discussion regarding how to approach dating is that of preparing practically. One of the greatest lies that we as Christians have believed is that we should not prepare to date. It is true that God has created marriage as a free gift for our benefit, but in our culture, we must view dating as the vehicle to obtain that end blessing. With this in mind, we must ask the question, "What am I doing today to prepare for dating tomorrow?" The importance of preparing today for tomorrow is that each tomorrow will bring you closer to walking down the aisle toward your future spouse.

The church has found itself in a bad place. Christian men and women are engaging in dating with little to no preparation. In comparison to the life of an everyday teenager, this lack of training is astounding. Many students today are involved in a variety of athletics, clubs, and organizations. A common thread exists between high school musicians, athletes, actors, and the FFA club. Actually, a single word weaves these diverse groups together: preparation. Each of these groups prepares its members for something, somewhere, at some time.

An athlete prepares to compete in an event on a certain date. A musician prepares to perform their music at a recital, concert, or audition on a certain day and time. These practices and rehearsals are the scheduled regimen for preparing to read and play music, shoot a basketball, or even perform a square dance. Likewise, Christian teenagers should prepare for the date. The subject matter of relating to a potential future mate is far too costly, significant, and God-ordained to simply "learn as we go" and not put our heart, mind, and soul to the task of understanding them. So how do we prepare for dating?

The apostle Paul wrote to his younger protégé Timothy, saying, "Let no one despise you for your youth, but set the believers an example in speech, in conduct, in love, in faith, in purity" (1

Tim. 4:12). I love this verse because it is like listening to a coach talking to his player. Here, the coach is giving Timothy the "fundamentals speech." It is as if Paul is standing in the locker room using the chalkboard to remind his team that the basics are essential. Preparing is practicing, and practicing includes running the fundamentals again and again. What are these fundamentals? How do you prepare yourself for dating? The coach gives us a game plan for the dating game.

First, you pay attention to the words that come from your mouth. Are you setting an example to others, regardless of your age, that the words you use are life- giving, truthful, and honest? Words are an overflow of the heart (Luke 6:45). They have power to both give life and take it out of someone (Proverbs 18:21). Believe me, your words have tremendous power.

I still recall a fatal blow to my self-esteem in the form of a phrase issued toward me while I was walking down the hallway of my junior high school. In tandem step with my awkward, heavy-set frame strolled "the girl" I had a crush on. Next to her walked her friend. At one point, my secret crush turned to her female companion and asked, "So what do you think?" To this day, I have not forgotten the response to that question. Our third-wheel hallway companion looked at me, then looked at her friend and replied, "If you like them big." Immediately, my confidence was shaken. For years, ever since that moment, I have wrestled with my body image, struggling to find satisfaction and contentment with it. You will exchange many words in the dating game, and they will either make or break your current date—and your future marriage.

The next part of the game plan for preparing practically for dating includes paying attention to your actions. Do your actions match your words? James, the brother of Jesus, reminded Christians that faith without deeds or "conduct" was worthless and unable to save (James 2:14). Faith, if not accompanied by action, is a dead faith (2:17). Our actions, like our words, show us and others what is really in our hearts. It is not enough to talk the talk; we are also to walk the walk.

I am convinced that actions do not speak louder than words. Actions and words are equal in their attention-getting capabilities. However, actions give credibility to our words. A few years ago, I attempted to break a habit of sleeping later than I should. I used powerful words, communicating to my lovely wife that I was going to make a change! They were passionate, emotional, and very convincing declarations. However, with much love and truth, Hannah consistently reminded me that she would believe my sincerity when my actions began proving otherwise. It is one thing to say you are going to run a marathon. It is another thing to show up, run, and cross the finish line.

The unity between our words and actions speaks to our character and integrity. The Proverbs record that a righteous man, walking in his integrity, is a blessing to his children (Proverbs 20:7). Future generations in Western culture will trace their origin to a man and woman dating. Integrity in dating, then, sets a course of blessing that will result in future blessings to future generations.

A preparing Christian also sets an example by loving God and loving others. Life is about relationships. Love is at the foundation of every relationship. Jesus clarified the proper order of this love as God first and others second (Matthew 22:36-40). This love is extended to all people regardless of age, gender, occupation, and even religious belief. It is a love filled with grace and truth because it emulates the embodiment of God's love in the person and work of Jesus Christ. As you prepare for dating, are you following Jesus's example of sacrificial love toward your family, friends, teachers, classmates, and co-workers? At the end of the day, are you most concerned about yourself? Do you seek to serve others or serve yourself?

I'll never forget serving in Louisiana. A small subgroup of our mission team was tasked with the job of rewiring a home. Duly naming ourselves "Team Zap," I quickly found myself sweating, serving, and surviving brutal July humidity in New Orleans. Though the conditions were difficult, I look back on that experience with a smile. We embodied the mission of Jesus that summer by coming to serve and not to be served (Matthew 20:28). In reality, I was helping myself prepare for the date as well. By serving others, I was learning my future calling to serve my spouse and love her in the same way I would want to be loved. This practical reality of love and service on that trip emanated from a deeper desire to love God first and foremost in my life. If you want to date well, you have to love and serve God first, and others second.

A preparing dater also seeks to foster, exhibit, and maintain faith in God. The writer of Hebrews reminds us that without faith, no one can please God (Hebrews 11:6). It is impossible. Furthermore, the author says that the seeking follower of God must have a faith that believes in the existence of God and believes that God rewards those who seek Him. This leads us to an obvious concern regarding the validity of one's faith. Do you have a faith that believes God is real, personal, and seeks to reward you with grace through faith in Jesus Christ as your Lord and Savior? Do you believe you are in need of grace due to your sin, which separates you from God? Do you believe that God revealed His will and plan for your life within Scripture? An affirmative answer to these questions will indicate an affinity toward the things of God that will aid you in dating with humility, love, tenderness, and faith.

The final piece of the coach's game plan for preparing for dating is that of setting an example in the area of purity. In fact, it is this last example that leads us to our second principle. We will discuss purity in just a moment. However, before we get there, one final word about preparing for dating.

Do you know who always wins America's Got Talent? People who have prepared. People who have prepared practically, and set examples for others regarding the importance of, dedication to, and benefit of hard work. Sure, you can get on the show despite your lack of preparation, but you will not win the contest. Only the prepared perform well. If you want to win at dating, the good news is that God wants you to win as well. However, the way to win is always through preparation.

Pursue Purity

Dating has a bad habit of causing many Christians to throw out the pursuit of purity. It is common to hear phrases like "Netflix and Chill" today, alluding to inappropriate and illicit behavior. Attempting to purchase groceries today alerts the shopper to the importance of sexual technique as advertised by the latest magazine covers. Sex is a gift from God, with the purpose of being enjoyed when God gives it to you in the proper context of marriage. We will discuss sex more in a later chapter. However, pursuing purity goes far deeper than avoiding sexual relations before marriage.

Pursuing purity includes setting an example of fleeing sexual intimacy outside of the marriage bed. This includes fleeing from the temptations of lust and pornography. God desires for you to pursue purity, which will prepare you for dating and marriage.

It is strange to say, but the way to prepare for dating is to pursue purity. However, in order to pursue purity you have to flee from immorality. Let me say it in a more memorable and portable way: To pursue purity, you must run from *risky*. Running from risky is both biblical and sexy (have you ever used those two words in the same sentence?).

Running from risky is exactly what Joseph did. The Bible tells us Joseph was bought as a slave by Pharaoh's Captain of the Guard, Potiphar. God was with Joseph, and Joseph found favor in the sight of his Egyptian master. Everything Joseph was put in charge of succeeded because God blessed it. If that wasn't good enough, the Scripture also says, "...Now Joseph was handsome in form and appearance" (Gen. 39:6). If Joseph wasn't a slave, you would think he had it made. Good looking, successful, and his boss didn't worry about anything. Whatever his master owned, except for his wife, Joseph took care of and probably indulged in a bit as well.

Then the scene shifts, and it says his master's wife cast her eyes on Joseph, urging him to her bedroom. Joseph refused. Not only did he refuse once, but "day after day, he would not listen to her, to lie beside her or to be with her" (39:10). This refusal obviously made her want him even more, because she waited for the perfect moment. When no men were in the house, she cornered Joseph and took hold of his clothes. In that moment, Joseph made a decision to run from risky, and that is exactly what he did. "...But he left his garment in her hand and fled and got out of the house" (39:12). In order to pursue purity, you have to run from risky. You have to flee fornication.

Running from risky is a common theme throughout Scripture. The apostle Paul wrote to the Corinthian church saying, "Flee from sexual immorality. Every other sin a person commits is outside the body, but the sexually immoral person sins against his own body" (1 Cor. 6:18). In a similar vein, Paul also wrote to his young protégé Timothy, encouraging him to act like Joseph. He said, "So flee youthful passions and pursue righteousness, faith, love, and peace, along with those who call on the Lord from a pure heart" (2 Tim. 2:22).

You can see the obvious connection. To pursue purity means to flee from impurity. To pursue purity means to run from risky. However, it is a bit deeper than that. When Paul wrote to Timothy, notice he said to flee impurity and pursue something else. Pursuing purity is just that, a thoughtful effort to catch something. Are you truly trying to catch purity in your life? Or is it just a vague "I think I should," but when rubber hits the road, you never start running? I ask because I was there. There were times in my life where I would think, "I should not be doing this," but I struggled to start running. However, let me tell you something. What do you experience once you start running? It becomes easier. When you know that you are called by God to run away from risky and pursue purity, your finish line is clarified. When you know where you are running to, then you can figure out how to get there.

With our finish line of purity in mind, I want to examine how we can get there. I believe God has given us two "running shoes" to aid us in this pursuit of purity. Those running shoes include Scripture and the Holy Spirit. In addition, I believe God has given us people to run the race with us in order to catch purity. First, let's tie up our laces.

The first running shoe God has given us for pursuing purity is the Bible. Do you recall when Jesus was tempted by Satan? Jesus was led by the Spirit to into the wilderness in order to face a period of temptation by the Father of Lies. The purity of Jesus was only one of the facets of his life that was tempted in that desert, in an effort to thwart the plan of God for Jesus to be our sinless sacrifice.

Do you remember how Jesus responded to each temptation from the devil? He quoted Scripture. He upheld the truth of God's Word and quoted the Old Testament. Three times Jesus replied to Satan with the words, "It is written" before speaking the very words of God back to the Father of Lies. My favorite line is when Jesus spoke to the devil saying, "...Be gone, Satan! For it is written, 'You shall worship the Lord your God and him only shall you serve'" (Matt. 4:10).

We have the power to face our temptation with a sword of truth. It is this sword that has the power to cause Satan and his lies to flee from our hearts, minds, and souls. It is the power of the sword that causes Satan to "be gone" with his lies and temptations. The first running shoe we are given to pursue purity is that of truth. The Word of God is truth that cuts through the lies of Satan. This is why this entire talk is seasoned with teachings from the Bible. Hebrews 4:12 says, "For the word of God is living and active, sharper than any two-edged sword, piercing to the division of soul and of spirit, of joints and of marrow, and discerning the thoughts and intentions of the heart." The very words that Jesus quoted and the words that I have brought before you from Scripture are able to pierce and cut at your soul, exposing the lies of Satan and removing or cutting them away with truth.

I love that Paul reminds believers today that we have various pieces of armor given to us by God in order to withstand the attacks of the Evil One and his demonic forces. However, we often forget we are given just one weapon: "And take the helmet of salvation, and the sword of the Spirit, which is the word of God" (Eph. 6:17). We have the sword of the Spirit. It is sharp, living, and active. It is able to cut away the lies in order for truth to come in.

The second running shoe we have been given is the Holy Spirit. Scripture does the cutting while the Spirit does the convicting and leading. It is the Spirit of truth then that "...will guide you into all the truth..." (John 16:13), leading us to see the truth we need. Once truth is illuminated within the soul, the Spirit convicts the soul of where it has believed those lies. Jesus told his disciples that the Spirit would come after him and "convict the world concerning sin and righteousness and judgment; concerning sin, because they do not believe in Me" (John 16:8-9).

When the Spirit convicts us of sin, and perhaps of unbelief in Jesus, we then confess our sins and believe in the good news of the gospel. The Scriptures tell us "that if you confess with your mouth Jesus as Lord, and believe in your heart that God raised Him from the dead, you will be saved; for with the heart a person believes, resulting in righteousness, and with the mouth he confesses, resulting in salvation" (Rom. 10:9-10). After that confession, prompted by faith, salvation occurs. In that moment of confession and faith, the Spirit then takes residence within us

(Romans 8:11). It is this presence of the Spirit that begins to pro-
duce the fruits of salvation within our life. One of those fruits is
self-control (Galatians 5:23). Every time you pursue purity, it is
the direct result of the Holy Spirit working in your life.

I love the imagery that Paul uses in Galatians 5. He describes
this relationship with the third member of the Godhead as "walking by the Spirit." For our purposes, let's say "run by the Spirit"
in your pursuit of purity. The Bible says that when you lace up
the Spirit of truth, you "will not carry out the desire of the flesh"
(Gal. 5:16).

Finally, God has given us people with whom to run our race in
life. These people spur us on to continue pursuing purity and not
give up until we cross the finish line. Even a quick, cursory look
at the Scriptures reminds us of the importance of people and relationships. Life is all about relationships, after all.

We are to live in relationship with God and with other people
(Matthew 22:36-40). We were made to live in relationship with
other human beings, and it is not good for mankind to be alone
in this life (Genesis 2:18). People sharpen each other, making
each other better because of close proximity (Proverbs 27:17).
Believers are to "stir up one another to love and good works"
as we meet together and encourage one another (Hebrews
10:24-25). There is a clear theme in Scripture of people living
in relationship with one another and making each other sharper
through love, accountability, and encouragement. Jesus told his
disciples to follow him, and he would make them disciple mak-
ers. The apostle Paul would establish churches by raising up a
number of elders to lead the congregation. Just as God the Father
is a community between the Son and the Holy Spirit, so we are
made likewise in His image for community with others, both
God and people (Genesis 1:26).

Each of us needs other believers surrounding us who are running the same direction we are. When I am surrounded by a
group of like-minded young men and women, I am all the more

motivated to move in the same direction they are. Likewise, you need to surround yourself with people pursuing purity and running from risky. It is much easier to finish a marathon when you have others encouraging you and cheering you on.

Pray Purposefully

The third principle for approaching dating is the importance of prayer, and praying with purpose. It is easy for us to believe that God does not hear our prayers. However, if He did not hear our prayers, Jesus would never have told us to go into our rooms to pray. It is in the secret place of a chair, a bedroom, or even a car that "...your Father who sees in secret will reward you" (Matt. 6:6). That reward is an answer to our prayers. God hears our prayers and God answers them. However, the answers to our prayers are never according to our will but according to the will of God.

1 John 1:14-15 says, "And this is the confidence we have toward him, that if we ask anything according to his will he hears us. And if we know that he hears us in whatever we ask, we know that we have the requests that we have asked of him."

This then leads us to the conclusion that if you are interested in dating, you'd better start praying. Start asking God to show you the right person and the right time to begin dating. (Just a quick side note: the right time coincides with your parents giving you permission to begin dating. If you don't believe they have that right, we will discuss your role in the family at a later time.)

God will answer your prayer concerning the right time to date and the right person to date. God answers prayers. I remember sitting around four tables in our monthly all-staff meeting. At Cool Spring Baptist Church, we have a rather large staff. Our lead pastor invited everyone seated around the table to share one answered prayer and one unanswered prayer. It took over an hour to hear both answered and unanswered prayers. I remember chills going down my spine hearing of prayers from the people of God being met by the will of God and coming to fruition. It was amazing. I was one of many staff members who thanked Pastor Brad for inviting us into this rather easy but awe-inspiring exercise of witnessing God's faithfulness to answer prayer according to a divine plan.

I remember praying for my future spouse. In fact, I pray every night for my daughter's future spouse. Why wait? My prayer for my wife was a prayer born out of frustration and confusion. Just before I had begun praying that prayer, I was dumped by a girl I met through an online dating platform. She was confused, I was confused, and thankfully God answered that prayer of confusion with an affirmative, "No, do not date her."

With that resolved, I remember signing off one internet dating platform and praying, "God, I only want to date the woman you have planned for me." Little did I know, only fifteen miles down the road from my apartment, my future wife was praying those exact words. I will tell you more of that story later.

Practice Patience

We live in a culture of "I want it now"—and many things are delivered within that time frame. Packages are shipped within two days. Fast food is a steady part of many diets. Movies and music are streamed instantly. Dating apps even match users with members of the opposite sex upon payment for their services, allowing instant communication with potential matches. However, impatience in dating will only cause pain and frustration. Choosing your future spouse requires preparation, purity, and prayer. It also requires patience.

Patience is one component of the fruit of the Spirit (Galatians 5:22). That is to say, if the Spirit resides within you, patience should find practice in your life. The people of God are those loved and chosen by God who then clothe themselves with compassion, kindness, humility, gentleness, and patience (Colossians 3:12).

I believe God will listen to your prayers regarding dating when you are ready to learn and exhibit patience. Please hear that I am saying God will listen to your prayers through your patience. He will answer them according to the divine plan, based on God's timing, and not your plan or your timing. The reason I think this is because of what the psalmist says: "I waited patiently for the Lord's help; then he listened to me and heard my cry" (Ps. 40:1). Notice the writer describes his experience of God listening to his cries after the psalmist "waited patiently."

A lot of questions surround dating. *Whom should I date?* Wait patiently, God will answer. *When should I begin dating?* Wait patiently, God will answer. By the way, sometimes that answer comes through parents. You are called to honor and obey their decisions for your life, which include permission for and boundaries around dating (Ephesians 6:1-4; Colossians 3:20). Be patient, trust me. If you are not, you may make the wrong decision.

You never want to settle for less, and yet that is what many do. They settle for the girl who strings them along for years. They settle for the guy who is never around. They settle for split custody over the kids. They settle for a an unbelieving spouse, and a lifetime of difficulty. They settle for less than what God desires for them.

We know many people who have dated at the wrong time and with the wrong person. In fact, Hannah and I have ourselves dated the wrong people at the wrong time in order to speed along God's timing. Reasons abound for these inevitable, fiery crashes of hormones, emotions, and expectations. At times, it is sin and temptation that play a large part in these failures. Satan and his demons also influence relationships for their destruction. Apprehensive and unprepared parents, or even negligible and oblivious parents are responsible to a degree as well. Even our culture, Christian or not, often influences people to commit to others at a young age and take relationships too fast and too extreme. These factors all play into an onslaught of unexpected pregnancy, lost virginity, patterns of casual and sinful sex, and broken relationships.

This is the danger of impatience. When you reject the importance of patience, the consequences are inevitable, hurtful, and costly. You may even find yourself married to the wrong person. It is not the will of God for a believer to marry an unbeliever (2 Corinthians 6:14). Some make this mistake out of impatience. When that happens, it is like attempting to lock eyes with someone driving in the opposite direction. (Thank you, Andy Stanley, for that analogy.) It is very difficult for the two of you to head in the same direction together. This is not to say your marriage is doomed or that God has abandoned you, but your calling will be to witness to your spouse first and foremost. That avenue of life will take much prayer, patience, blood, sweat, and tears.

When you accept the power of patience, you decide to make eye contact with someone driving in the same direction as you. In fact, you may even devote seven years to your future spouse, as in the story of Jacob working seven years in order to marry Rachel (Genesis 29:15-30). As the story turned out, he worked fourteen years in total for his uncle Laban in order to marry the woman of his dreams. That is called patience.

Alright, so back to my wife and me. After we both prayed for our future spouses, God began weaving a story that could only give glory, honor, and praise to His will. At the age of twenty-two, I began my first full-time student ministry at LifePointe Christian Church in Toano, VA. About two months into my ministry, I was ready to start dating. However, I was uninterested in dating anyone at the church. So, like any good millennial, I tried an online dating platform. It ended in a breakup. Then, I prayed for God to guide my steps. After that prayer, I logged onto a second online dating platform. The will of God became clear. His grace abounds, and it manifested in the woman Hannah Abigail—whose name means "grace" in Hebrew, by the way.

She was perfect. Beautiful, fun-loving, and family- oriented. Her online profile even listed faith as her priority above all else. I decided to send an email inviting her to lunch, my treat of course. I told her to pick her favorite restaurant. An email from this mystery woman returned my request with an affirmative. The date was set. Then, a second email journeyed into my inbox. It read, "I have a funny story to tell you." I was confused, intrigued, and scared all at once.

Although we met in April, Hannah's story started in October. A few weeks after I started serving at LifePointe, Hannah was approached by a woman in our church, Trish. At the time, Hannah was coaching swimming at the local YMCA. A mom with kids on Hannah's swim team mentioned, "You need to dump your boyfriend because I met your husband." Tactful to say the least. Laughing off the suggestion, Hannah was flattered but not exactly sold. She was in a relationship. In fact, at the time, she was considering taking another serious step with the relationship.

Time passed. I was still dating online. Hannah's relationship with her boyfriend ended. Praise God! Somewhere along the line, at swim practice, Trish heard the juicy news of Hannah's new relationship status and burst into the YMCA office. She blurted out, "Why didn't you tell me you broke up with your boyfriend?! You need to come to our church and meet our youth pastor. Brian (Trish's husband) even agrees with me and he never supports me in my matchmaking." Well, it is a little hard to say no to Trish. So, Hannah agreed to come and visit. A date was set, unbeknownst to me, and Hannah was scheduled to attend LifePointe Christian Church in May of 2014. It gets a little crazier, trust me.

Hannah has a friend named Felicia. She had just recently come out of a relationship. In the midst of Trish's attempt at matchmaking, Felicia (who was also Hannah's roommate) asked Hannah to sign up for Match.com with her. Hannah was skeptical at first.

To support her friend, she agreed to sign up for a free profile. She was so skeptical about online dating that she refused to pay for the premium service. Felicia, however, was all in. She chose the premium service. After all, Hannah's mom had met her husband on Match.com and she had encouraged Felicia to try the service. Yes, you read right. Hannah's mom did a better job of selling Hannah's roommate on the service than she did her own daughter. Hannah went along with it only because of the time-honored tradition of girls doing things together!

So Hannah set up her online profile just as a favor to Felicia. Immediately, her email was flooded with solicitations to purchase the further services of Match.com. To this day, she swears she was simply swipe-deleting the emails in her inbox when her phone glitched. It just so happened to open an email addressed to her from Derek Nicksich. Now, get this. I had sent an email to an unknown woman because her profile interested me, a profile that stated God was a priority in her life. This unknown woman already knew who I was, and was planning to meet me in only a few weeks. This unknown woman prayed the same prayer I had prayed, only fifteen miles away from me, before I ever sent her an email. This unknown woman set up an account on Match.com, the same website I'd moved on to try, not because she wanted to but because her friend asked her to try it with her. Her phone glitched and opened my email in the midst of deleting others. Only God could orchestrate such an intricate web of connection to fulfill the divine purpose of bringing two of His children together into holy matrimony. I write this now, as we are looking to purchase our second home, with our second child on the way, beginning our second student ministry in Mechanicsville, VA. God is a God of second chances, even if you have made some tremendous dating mistakes. And trust me, both Hannah and I have.

This is my goal for you, to recognize that God is a God of second chances. It doesn't matter if you have made mistakes in dating. It is not the divine plan for you to share a dating fail story. It is the will of God for you to share an intricate, glorious, and "Only God could orchestrate this" kind of story. In order to do that, I believe God wants you to do a few things first.

In order not to fail in dating, God wants you to prepare practically. In order to not to fail in dating, God wants you to pursue purity. In order not to fail in dating, God wants you to pray purposefully. In order not to fail in dating, God wants you to practice patience patiently.

Dating is awkward when God is left out. Dating is also dangerous when God is left out. God desires for you to succeed before you date, during your date, and after your date. I do as well. When you relate well on the date, you just might find your mate. My dream for you is that you would date well by following the principles God has laid out for you. Let's kick awkward out, save the birds, and invite God into our relationships. When you do that, not only will the birds live, but your dating life will not die a miserable death. Instead, your dating life will lead you to live the life God desires for you, in marriage to the woman or man picked for you by God.

Talk About It

1. Take a few moments of self-assessment. Do you believe your dating life invites God into the process or leaves him out?

2. How important is preparation in life? Why do you think many Christians forget that dating needs preparation as well?

3. God hears our requests and answers them according to His will (1 John 1:14-15). How does this encourage you to begin praying about dating?

4. This chapter discusses running from risky, or pursuing purity. What practical step can you take today to pursue purity in your life, and in your dating relationships?
5. Describe areas in your life where patience is a struggle. Within those areas, what are some of the consequences that have occurred due to impatience? What are the potential consequences of being impatient in dating?
6. Were you encouraged hearing the story of Hannah and Derek meeting? How does their story point to the goodness of God in dating?

Do It

1. This week, work at incorporating these four principles into your life.
2. Examining the four principles, which are you currently applying to your life in areas other than dating? Is it easier to apply these principles to your life outside of dating?
3. If you are dating, evaluate the relationship you are in and seek to incorporate these four principles into your current relationship. If the other member of your relationship is not receptive to these principles, seek advice from an older, wiser Christian mentor.
4. Consider bringing a mentor into your dating relationship to meet with you and your significant other regularly.
5. If you are not dating, consider enlisting a mentor to help you prepare practically for Christian dating.
6. **For Parents, Small Group Leaders, and Pastors**: Consider how you can teach your child or group where you have succeeded and where you have not succeeded in these four principles. With wisdom and discernment, use your dating wins and fails in the past as examples to share with your group/child.

RIGHT NOW

What I am about to tell you is true. It is the story of a middle school boy who found himself in trouble rather unexpectedly. Shocker, right? It all went down at youth group.

For the purposes of telling our story, let's call this boy Austin. So, it was a Wednesday night and Austin found himself talking to Taylor at youth group. Just your ordinary, average middle school boy-girl conversation. From a distance, to the adult eye, it might seem innocent, and possibly even awkward.

At some point in the conversation, the awkward and innocent turned illicit. Austin proceeded to pull a handwritten note from his backpack's side pocket and hand it to Taylor. His words were explicit: "Don't show this to anyone." His instructions continued, "You can read it later." Within the note, Austin alluded to an attraction he had toward another girl at school, Nicole. Taylor and Austin were both friends of Nicole, but Taylor was closer to her. The note was more than a mere love profession, but a rendezvous confession about a potential meeting with Nicole that was supposedly scheduled to occur in the near future. Austin told Taylor about how he intended to kiss Nicole at this love-riddled reunion.

When confronted about the truth of this story, it turned out it was all made up from the start. I know this boy had no such secret mission planned, but telling someone else about it with the words, "Don't show this to anyone" reminds me of every evil villain revealing his plan to the hero just before good wins in the end. Well, here is how Austin's evil plan was thwarted.

By the grace of God, the note found its way into the hands of an adult at the church. The note was then promptly handed to the boy's parents. Austin's father was a prominent leader in the church and he was not only embarrassed by the note; he was also infuriated with his son. He proceeded to scold his son at home, forgetting constructive criticism or biblical reproof. As described, "It was like hearing a broken record stuck on the same lines over and over again." Austin's dad kept saying, "Not good Austin, this is not good." He would pace back and forth saying, "This is not good," as his pitch climbed higher and his face turned redder.

At some point in the father-son conversation, Austin was able to excuse himself upstairs, heading to his room. Slinking up the steps, he crossed the threshold of his room, gently closing the door. Lying down on his bed, he fell asleep, thinking things could not get any worse. They did. His mother came upstairs, seeing the closed door, and proceeded to slide a pamphlet on teen purity under the door. No conversation or explanation, just a speedy delivery. Waking up from his sleep and attempting to get ready for school, Austin found the pamphlet and read the cover. Already uncomfortable from the previous excitement with the note and his father, the pamphlet made him feel only worse and even more awkward. Taking the booklet, he gently placed it on the bookshelf, unread, and went back to bed.

My fear for you is that any and all discussion concerning the word "sex" has been placed on the shelf or slid under the door by either you, your parents, or even worse, the church. It seems that many students today are recounting similar experiences. Awkward conversations about "the birds and the bees" with little to no benefit. Meanwhile, detailed sex seminars are occurring on the school playground, the bus ride home, a streaming app, or a simple Google search.

The greatest tragedy occurs when the church, proprietor of God's truth, places one of the greatest gifts from God on the shelf because it makes us feel awkward and uncomfortable. The travesty is found when a gift from God, like sex, collects dust in our conversations and then loses respect in our minds because we as

Christians do not understand it or talk about it. Sex becomes the elephant in the room that no one addresses and many have vastly different opinions about—often unbiblical ones.

My Goal

With that in mind, my goal for you within this chapter is three-fold:

1. I want you to understand and believe that sex is a gift from God.
2. I want you to understand and believe that this gift is to be opened when the giver gives it.
3. I want you to understand that sex is good when "right
 • now" is right.

That's my outline. Sex is a gift from God. This gift is opened when the giver gives us the gift. Makes sense, right? Sex is a good gift, a great gift in fact, but only when "right now" is right. I hope you know that I care enough about you, and the truth of God's Word, to share this with you. I don't want the words "sex" and "awkward" to find themselves in the same sentence for you. I want you to enjoy the gift of sex. However, in order to enjoy it you need to understand it, and know when to use it.

Having said this, we need to start in Genesis 2. Within the creation account, we read of God forming a man from the dust of the ground. Breathing life into his nostrils, God made the man a living creature (2:7). Adam, as the text later names him, was given a job description: official groundskeeper in God's garden.

To say the garden of Eden was beautiful is an understatement. The book of Genesis describes this garden as paradise. It says "every tree that is pleasant to the sight and good for food" existed in this nature reserve (2:9). A river flowed in and through the garden, where precious metals and minerals were also found.

It was there, in paradise, that God placed Adam "to work it and keep it" (2:15).

However, within a matter of sentences, paradise is lacking. Genesis tells us God said, "It is not good that the man should be alone; I will make him a helper fit for him" (2:18). So, somewhere along the line, Adam was naming the livestock and the birds, but began to get tired. So God caused a deep sleep to occur, and Adam took a nap. While Adam slept, God performed surgery, taking a rib from Adam's side and closing up the place with flesh (2:21). That's why your side hurts when you eat too many tortilla chips at a Mexican restaurant. No, I'm just kidding.

Using that rib, God delicately "made into a woman and brought her to the man" (2:22). Waking up, Adam took one look at this new creature and said, "Whoa, man." Sorry, preacher jokes. So there you have it. The first creation of man and woman. I know what you are thinking: "So what does this have to do with sex?" Everything. Trust me.

When we look at Genesis 2, we understand and read with rather easy comprehension that Eve, the woman, was a helper to Adam. She was a gift to Adam. It was not good for man to be alone, according to God (2:18). So, the solution to this problem was the gift of a helper, a friend, courtesy of the Creator.

In the first few chapters of Genesis, we see that God is a giver. The gifts of God littered the garden of Eden. Natural sugars abounded in every fruit imaginable. Fresh, clear spring water flowed through the garden, providing drinking water that beat any bottled water. Animals abounded, gifts of love and companionship. Plants were gifts for both enjoying their colors and eating their fruits.

Needless to say, the gift of life for Adam was the greatest gift of all, followed only by the creation of Eve as a companion. God is a God of gift giving. Not only does Genesis declare this, but so does the New Testament. James, the brother of Jesus, wrote,

"Every good gift and every perfect gift is from above, coming down from the Father of lights..." (James 1:17).

After the gift of Eve was given to Adam, another gift was created in the process. Genesis 2:24 says, "Therefore a man shall leave his father and his mother and hold fast to his wife, and they shall become one flesh." With these few simple words, another gift was given to both Adam and Eve—that of marriage.

Within their new union, Adam and Eve found themselves married. The institution of marriage is the process by which one man and one woman leave their respective parents and begin their own family.

Within that declaration of marriage, of the new institution that would find itself passed down from generation to generation, yet another gift was presented. When a man and woman are married, they "become one flesh" (2:24). In other words, they begin to enjoy the gift of deep physical and relational intimacy together. In other words, they enjoy the gift of sex given to them by God.

The Gift of Sex

Sex is a gift from God. We need to state that, believe it, and remember it. If sex is a gift from God, it also means that it is a good gift (James 1:17). It is the gift of pleasure, intimacy, and connection between spouses. It also enables the possibility of producing children. Isn't that amazing? The gift of marriage brings the gift of sex, which brings about the possible gift of children. The New Living Translation says, "Children are a gift from the Lord; they are a reward from him" (Ps. 127:3).

Now think with me about the endless gifts from God. First, we see the gift of life. Then, the gift of nature. Adam is given life. Animals are given names, gifts from Adam. Eve is given life, to accompany Adam. Marriage is given to the both of them. Sex is given to Adam and Eve in the context of marriage. The possibility of a family is given to Adam and Eve, who would later have children, because the gift of sex creates the possibility for further gifts of children.

God is clearly a giver of gifts. We must think, believe, and articulate to one another that every gift of God is good. That is to say, we must think, believe, and tell one another that sex is a gift from God. Sex is a good gift, a great gift, from an equally good and great God.

I like to think of sex like a driver's license. Bear with me. Your license to drive is essentially a gift from the state department to you. It is a gift that has certain benefits prescribed to it. When you are given this gift, you are able to operate a motor vehicle. Operating a car allows you to drive at all hours of the day, commuting to and from work and school. It also allows you to take road trips, go on vacation, or visit friends and family.

However, this gift carries with it certain requirements and responsibilities. You are required by the state to meet certain qualifications before receiving the license. If you fail to meet those qualifications, you are inhibited from enjoying the gift to its fullest. Furthermore, if you illegally bypass those qualifications, you are endangering others and preventing them from enjoying the gift of driving to its fullest potential. There are rules for you to follow, and if you abuse those rules you can harm yourself and other people.

Sex is like that. Sex is a gift from God, a good gift, that carries certain blessings and privileges. However, its box is stamped "fragile" and responsible handling is required. If it is not handled responsibly, there are grave consequences. This leads us to the question, "How does God want us to handle the gift of sex responsibly?"

When the Giver Gives

God wants us to enjoy the gift of sex. In order to do this responsibly, we must enjoy the gift of sex when the giver gives it to us. A gift is opened when it is received. In other words, a gift is opened when the giver gives it.

Birthdays roll around once a year. I know, that was a groundbreaking statement. When I grew up, my birthday came around on April 26, and my parents presented me with gifts because of the date and its significance. In other words, I received a gift on the day that it was appropriate for me to open it. My parents, the gift givers, gave me the gifts when it was appropriate to open them.

I cannot recall a single time my parents gave me a gift, wrapped up and labeled for me, and then said "Now keep this in your room for the next two weeks before you can open it." That's not how it works. A gift is opened when the giver gives it. Gifts are given with the purpose of others opening them immediately.

God gave a man and a woman, in a garden, the gift of sex. That gift was presented to them when the appropriate day came—the wedding day. It is on the marriage day that a man and woman unwrap the gift of sex because it is the appropriate day and time for which God gave that gift to mankind to open and enjoy.

The reason sex is enjoyed within the gift of marriage is because the order of the gifts indicates it. A man leaves his family, and clings to his wife. The term "wife" indicates that this man is now married to this woman. So it is that marriage precedes the man and woman becoming "one flesh." The marriage vows happen before physical intimacy. The ceremony concludes before the sex begins.

God's design for mankind is to enjoy the gift of marriage first, which then brings the gift of sex with it. Sex outside of marriage between one man and one woman, or any other combination, is simply not the gift of God. If any other arrangement of sex outside of a marriage between one man and woman is not the gift of God, it is therefore not good either, because only the gifts of God are good. Only sex within the confines of marriage is the proper gift of God. This leads us to the question, "When am I ready to marry?"

The answer is, when you are able. Now, let me qualify that statement. Able indicates an ability to care for yourself. Able means holding down a job, paying your bills, and not being dependent on your parents.

Able indicates that your physical needs are met by your own hands. Isn't that what Genesis 2 implies? A man leaves his family, and the care his family provides, to begin a new family. Within that new family, the husband and wife take on new roles of providing, cherishing, and child-rearing together. It also indicates that the physical needs of others are met by your own hands. That is when you are ready to receive the gift of marriage, and the subsequent gift of sex after marriage. May I refer you back to our first chapter, on dating? The right time is when you believe it is the right time for you to pursue a relationship with a man or woman with the intention of marriage.

God gave the gift of sex to Adam and Eve to enjoy on their own, after they had been married. A gift is enjoyed when the giver gives it. Likewise, the Christian faith upholds the design of God for enjoying the gift of sex, after the wedding vows, within the context of the marriage bed.

Have you ever asked the question, where does the Bible say sex before marriage is wrong? I know I asked that question often as a teenager. Let me point you to 1 Corinthians 7:2, which says, "But because of the temptation to sexual immorality, each man should have his own wife and each woman her own husband." In other words, the Bible says sex within a husband-and-wife relationship is not a temptation, but a gift. It is sex outside of marriage that is a temptation. The term "sexual immorality" also alludes to any sexual activity, from lust to fornication; pornography to fooling around.

1 Thessalonians 4:3-5 states, "For this is the will of God, your sanctification: that you abstain from sexual immorality; that each one of you know how to control his own body in holiness and honor, not in the passion of lust like the Gentiles who do not know God..." It is the will of God for you to look like Jesus. That is the essential understanding of sanctification. Jesus abstained from sexual immorality, and God desires us to do the same.

Part of that abstinence is learning to control our bodies and not facilitating lust in our lives. It is this rejection, this abstaining, that is the result of the Spirit working in our lives. Self-control honors God and fulfills His will in our lives. In other words, God commands us to control our bodies and to only open the gift of sex within the gift of marriage. When you do that, God is pleased. When you do that, you enjoy the gift from the giver in the right way and at the right time. When you do that, blessing occurs.

One of the greatest challenges in your life is learning self-control. Learning how to control your body is tantamount to fulfilling the will of God. I am growing in this area. My wife plays a pivotal part in keeping my diet relatively healthy. She also lovingly reminds me when my portion sizes or food choices are not ideal. We eat "living foods" and drink plenty of water.

However, my struggle is on Tuesday mornings. I walk into our staff meeting and donuts litter the table. Two, sometimes three, boxes of donut holes are scattered around, only an arm's length away from my mouth. I brace myself for the inquiries from my fellow staff members, "Donut?" I think to myself, "No, I am good." Then I think, "Well, you know, one won't hurt." After I eat one, I begin to think, "Ok, I will limit myself to two." What's two times two? Four. Four times four? Well, it hasn't been that bad. Yet. Oh, and I won't mention the cookies that were brought to the work room one day. Then, there was leftover birthday cake, and more cookies upstairs! You get the idea. Self-control is important.

We all have our self-control battles, but notice that our self-control issues all involve our bodies to one degree or another. Our bodies are affected, but our soul is engaged in the process as well. Self-control is a soul issue as much as a bodily battle. James describes the passions within us that rage against the flesh and cause difficulties amongst others and ourselves (James 4:1). It is the will of the giver for us to control our desire to get.

Did you know that in the garden of Eden, man's ideal habitat in God's creation, there were restrictions? Adam and Eve were told to exhibit self-control. They were told not to eat of one tree. The reason for that restriction was their own good. When you receive your driver's license, not only do you receive the freedom to drive, but also the duty to obey restrictions on the road, including speed limits, red lights, and proper lanes. Those restrictions are for your good, and the good of others. Likewise, God has placed restrictions on when we should enjoy the gift of sex. It is only good, lawful, and legal according to God's law to open the good gift of sex when the giver gives it, and when right now is right.

When Right Now Is Wrong

This takes us to our final question. "What happens if right now is not right, but I still have sex?" Go with me to Genesis 25:24-34; I would like to tell you a story. We meet two twin boys, but they are as dissimilar as a toy poodle and a flying squirrel. Esau, the oldest, is born hairy and red. His name literally means hairy (very profound, I know). Jacob, the youngest by a hair, is grasping his brother's heel when the boys are born, symbolizing what would eventually happen between the two of them. They are born wrestling with one another. Fighting. Not getting along.

The boys grow up, and Esau becomes a rugged outdoorsman, a man of the field. Jacob, however, is more introverted. He stays inside, perhaps apt at organizing, tent making, and streamlining the livestock feeding process. One is a doer and the other a think-er. One is like Rocky Balboa, and the other is like Rain Man. One is like Hawkeye or the Green Arrow with a bow; the other is like Iron Man, the smart kid whose motto is "Work smarter not harder."

To complicate matters, the house is divided even further be-tween these two very different brothers. Isaac loves his son Esau because of the wild game he brings him to eat (25:28). However, Jacob is loved more by Rebekah. It is a house divided, and it is barely standing.

One day, Jacob is inside taking a cooking class. As he nears the conclusion of his YouTube tutorial, Esau comes in after a long day of hunting, beat tired. He cries out to his brother, "Give me some food because I am tired!" The hunter is hungry, but the hunter becomes the hunted. Seeing his opportunity, the young-er brother coils in wait, ready to strike. "Sell me your birthright now," he says (25:31).

Now, for our understanding, the birthright was the divine blessing of God on your life. Traditionally, the oldest son would receive the birthright, including a double portion of the inher-itance and spiritual leadership or headship of the family. Esau chooses, in a moment, to disdain what is his by right. Esau choos-es "right now" to trade away the will of God for his life. He lacks self-control and devalues the gift from God that a birthright is and says, "I am so hungry that I may even die, what use is this birthright to me?" (25:32).

Jacob's subtle moves are snakelike and cunning. "Swear to me now," he says, and so Esau swears his birthright to Jacob.

Did you notice the irony here? Right now, in a moment, for a bowl of soup, Esau rejects the blessing of God. For a bowl of soup, Esau chose "right now" instead of a double portion of di-vine blessing. Esau chose one meal, just one, in exchange for a God-given right. He received one bowl of food for a God-given blessing. He swapped a moment for the material.

You and I are faced with a similar choice. Will we choose "right now" over the blessing of God? When it comes to sex, "right now" is not worth selling the blessing of God on your life. Don't misunderstand me: if you have sex before marriage, you are not worthless to God or unredeemable. Not at all. That is the beauty of the gospel. It is good news to those who need good news. All of us have bad news, sin, and mistakes in our life. All of us have acted like Esau in one way or another.

The lesson for us is that "right now," acting without self-control, is not worth selling the unique gifts and blessings that God has for our lives. Each and every day you have "right now" moments and decisions that directly affect seeing the provision and blessing of God on your life. When you log onto the computer, you have "right now" decisions to make regarding your online integrity. When you find yourself alone with your significant other, you have "right now" decisions regarding maintaining your relational and sexual integrity before God until you are married.

May I simply say to you that right now is not worth "right now" unless right now is the right time. A bowl of soup is never worth more than the blessing of God on your life. I know that there are hundreds of people reading this book who have "right now" moments flashing before their eyes. May you know that you are not too far gone, and you are not alone.

However, God wants you to pursue the birthright of blessing on your life over those "right now" moments. There is a better way of living instead of succumbing to internet porn. There are those of you who are choosing to pressure that girl into sexual promiscuity because you think "right now" is worth more than what God has in store. Some of you are allowing a boy to pressure you and are therefore succumbing to his desires for you to forego the gift of sex, within the gift of marriage, because "right now" is more important to him. Don't chase a cheap thrill, and later despise the act. Listen to me. Does this describe you? There is hope for you. There is good news for you, for Jesus Christ was pierced for our transgressions. In other words, He was crushed and punished for our "right now" moments. The punishment that brought us peace right now, in this moment, was placed on him in that moment on the cross. When you place your faith and trust in Jesus Christ as Lord and Savior, your wounds are healed, your sins are forgiven, and you are welcomed into the loving arms of a man whose hands and side bear the punishment for your "right now" sin.

God hates your sin. God loves the one who commits the sin, so much so that He desires to redeem you in the area of sexual integrity and purity. You can find hope. You can find healing. You can find a new start. You can enjoy the gift of sex when the giver gives it. You can experience the blessing of when "right now" is right.

You have a choice right now regarding how you will move forward and address your "right now" temptations. Perhaps you need to confess your sin to God. The followers of Jesus are those who admit their sins (1 John 1:8), confessing them to God, and then find cleansing for them (1:9). That cleansing is found in the blood of Jesus (1:7).

After confessing our sins and believing in Jesus as our Lord and Savior and healer of our sins, followers of Jesus are called to begin a life of repentance. I think we often believe repentance means "I will no longer sin again." That is not true. However, repentance *is* a turning away from sin. It is a course correction for the trajectory of your life. You were heading in the wrong direction, and now you are turning the ship around. You were sinning against God, and now you are fighting against your sin because Jesus died for your soul.

Repentance leads you to begin a war against your sin. When Jesus spoke on the very subject of lust, he used a metaphor of tearing out the members of your body that cause you to sin. An eye, gone. A hand, cut off. Now, if you are fearfully and wonderfully made by the creator (Psalm 139), and that includes your eyes and hands, Jesus is not encouraging self-mutilation. God gave you your hands and eyes. The Son of God is using extreme word pictures to raise the level of seriousness we must place on fighting against sin and fleeing temptation. The principle behind the matter is that you must take any and all precautions to wage war against your sin. This is why the apostle Paul spoke in Ephesians 6 of taking up the armor of God and wielding the sword of truth, the Bible, against Satan's schemes. This is why John warned his readers that the world contains lusts of the flesh and eyes, and prideful temptations that are of this world and not of heaven (1 John 2:16). Satan is the ruler of this world and we are caught in the cross fire.

Finally, you must surround yourself with other believers who are headed in the same direction as you. You must flee from risky, and pursue purity. You may be reading this and think you are all alone in your struggles; you are not. In fact, I am going to list my email address at the back of this book in case you think you are alone. I promise, if you reach out to me, I will respond and do whatever I can to help you find a good group of Christians to aid you in experiencing "right now" at the right time.

The choice is yours. What will you do right now about "right now" in the future? No sinner is too far gone. No sexual sin is so heinous that the blood of Jesus cannot forgive it.

What will you do? Will you believe that sex is a gift from God? Will you believe that the gift of sex is intended to be opened when the giver gives the gift? Will you believe that sex is good when "right now" is right? Will you believe that God desires for you to exhibit self-control in this area of your life? Will you exchange the blessing of God on your life for a "right now" moment? How did that work out for Esau? Not too well. Will you exchange the blessing of God on your life for a bowl of soup, a cheap thrill, a feeling, a kiss, or will you believe that God's way is the best way? Will you believe that sex is good when "right now" is right, and when "right now" comes after the words, "I do"? The choice is yours.

Talk About It

1. How would you describe your experience with learning about sex?
2. When you read that every gift is from God above (James 1:17), is it difficult to believe that sex is a good gift from God? Why or why not?
3. "God wants us to enjoy the gift of sex. In order to do this responsibly, we must enjoy the gift of sex when the giver gives it to us." How is God's delivery time of sex different than what many other people believe?
4. Self-control is not only a fruit of the Spirit, but also the will of God for your sanctification. Explain areas in your life where you struggle with self-control.
5. What are some of the consequences of rejecting self-control and embracing sex outside of marriage?
6. We often trade blessings from God (provision, integrity, rewards) for bowls of soup (sin, addictions, struggles). Who are some of the people in your life who can hold you accountable regarding trading blessing for bowls; sanctification for soup?

Do It

1. Commit to reading a book or listening to a sermon series regarding God's design for sex.
2. Identify one or two people in your life that can hold you accountable to enjoying the gift of sex at the right time and in the right place.
3. Reach out to the person or people you identified as accountability partners and meet regularly, reading a book

or listening to a sermon series together and discussing it. End each meeting in prayer for one another.

FRIENDS FOREVER

Have you ever had a moment in time that you look back on and regret? I have too many to count. I would imagine you have at least one or two. Personally, one incident stands out in my mind. It happened in middle school, in either seventh or eighth grade. For our purposes, I am going to say it was seventh grade; I think that makes it sound a little more innocent. Defacing public property in seventh grade sounds better to me than doing so in eighth grade.

So, I am in seventh grade, and I walk into my English class, expecting our teacher to be sitting behind her desk. However, this day something was different. Behind the desk sat a woman I had never seen before. Yes, it was in fact a substitute teacher.

All my homies and cronies are high-fiving one another, thinking today is going to be a good day! Right? We're thinking today is a get-out-of-jail-free-card day. We envision no homework, but instead sitting and talking, or maybe even watching a movie. We might even rest our weary heads and catch up on some sleep.

Were we wrong. Our mystery woman greets our class, and then reveals a three ringed notebook bearing bad news. This was no, "I bring you good tidings of great joy" but "I bring you instructions for the class to your great demise." Our teacher had thought of everything, and there was much working, groaning, and not very much rejoicing.

Now, somewhere between the substitute teacher reading off our classroom instructions and my friends talking in front of me, I noticed the back seat of my chair was loose. Every time I leaned back, the seat would move thirty degrees and make a small clicking noise. Clicking noise, movement, and middle school students equals distraction. I was enthralled, engaged, and completely interested in this new development. Sitting in the back row of the class, I also had the advantage of the teacher not hearing my noisy fidgeting.

I made my friends aware of the situation, to their delight. At that moment, someone somewhere within my gaggle of cronies blurted out the words, "Break it off!"

At this point in the story, I think a point of clarification is necessary: I was not an obedient follower of Jesus Christ in seventh grade. I also would like to point out that defacing public property was not my idea, even though I eventually went through with it. It just makes me feel better saying that, all right? I was not the criminal mastermind, just the brute force.

With the power of peer pressure and presence tempting my adolescent faith, I attempted to lean back hard and break off the back of my chair. However, it was firmly attached and therefore I needed a new game plan. At this point, someone (again, not me) blurted out, "Kick it off" to which I humbly obliged.

Waiting until the teacher turned her back to the class in order to write on the chalkboard, I stood up and placed two hands on the desks in front of mine. I then proceed to hoist my legs off of the ground, placing all weight and momentum on my arms. Getting a brisk walking start, I timed my momentum just right to dropkick the back of the chair, channeling every fiber of my love for professional wrestling. (Yes, I said it. I loved professional wrestling.)

BOOM! It sounded like a gun went off. The back of the chair hit the floor and reverberated around the school. I remember hearing people from different classrooms on both floors talk about "that loud noise" they heard on the second floor in the morning. As I kicked the chair, I was able to simultaneously sit down in my seat and turn toward the blackboard just as the substitute teacher turned back from it to face the class. Locating the source of the noise, she noticed a group of eyes looking at the remnants of a school desk in the back row. There I sat, hands folded, with an expression of surprise on my face.

I didn't get in trouble, but I remember being so overcome with guilt that I walked into my teacher's classroom early in order to apologize. I didn't admit that I broke the chair, but I apologized for it breaking. Clearly, I was more afraid of getting in trouble than interested in confessing my sin. From that point on, I inherited a nickname by a few of my friends, "Dropkick Nicksich." It even found itself onto my video game systems as a label for when I played online with those same friends.

Defacing public property in seventh grade and lying about it was just one of my many sins for which Jesus Christ died on the cross. I share that story to say this: We all have moments in our lives where we regret an action, a word, or even a relationship with a boy or girl. When I look back on that moment, I regret my action and my words denying the truth.

I have shared that story before and made a similar point, but recently I discovered there is a far more prevalent truth embedded within it. The people you surround yourself with have profound influence on you. People influence you. I defaced public property and lied about my actions and words because one person told me to do it. I even found a semblance of identity in a sinful, destructive, and disrespectful moment, which I proudly wore online and in person as a nickname. People will influence you, for better or for worse.

Temple University funded a research program identifying the differences in brain activity when adolescents are alone versus when they are with their friends.[2] The specific focus of this study surrounded their ability to make decisions. At the end of the study, the researchers concluded that the mere presence of other people around them promoted more risk-taking in the lives of teenagers. Forget words—just the *presence* of peers promoted risky behavior.

They proved this conclusion by conducting an experiment with students between the ages of fourteen and eighteen. Teenagers were asked to play a driving simulation game on a computer. If participants completed the simulation, they were rewarded with cash prizes. The rules of the game were simple. Cash prizes were rewarded for completing the driving simulation in a certain amount of time. Players made decisions regarding how to handle yellow lights: race through them, or stop and wait for a green light. The dilemma is obvious, as speeding through them increases your likelihood of crashing but also shortens your time frame in which to finish the game. The sooner the finish time, the greater increase in your possible reward. In other words, you've got to risk it to get the biscuit. Well, you get more if you bet more. You also lose more. What would you do? The results were fascinating.

They discovered that high school students playing the driving simulation game alone would run fewer yellow lights and had fewer crashes in the game. However, when the researchers would tell the students that their friends, who had accompanied them to the study, were watching them play from the next room, the statistics drastically changed. When students were aware of peers watching them, they ran approximately forty percent more yellow lights. These drivers also crashed sixty percent more than players with no peer pressure.

I am thankful for science. It often proves exactly what God reveals to us through special revelation within Scripture. People have the power to influence us, and God has articulated that from the beginning of time. It is this very power to influence, coerce, tempt, and steer off course that calls for us to take note of the people we surround ourselves with.

The psalmist writes that the blessed man "walks not in the counsel of the wicked, nor stands in the way of sinners, nor sits in the seat of scoffers" (Ps. 1:1). Notice how a blessed man avoids the counsel, behavior, or attitude of certain people. Wise people understand the power of influence that others can wield, so they examine and analyze the people around them. They refuse to walk in a way that is contradictory to a wise way of living.

In the book of Proverbs, the author speaks of the great influence an adulterous woman has on men. He encourages his son to keep a path far from her and not to approach her house (Proverbs 5:8). Proverbs 13:20 says, "Whoever walks with the wise becomes wise, but the companion of fools will suffer harm." It is a simple principle, that who you surround yourself with will influence you. If you find friends who are wise and who follow Jesus, you will most likely become wise and follow Jesus as well.

The people you surround yourself with will have tremendous influence on you because they will either influence you to look like our Lord and Savior Jesus Christ, or they will influence you to run away from him entirely. If you surround yourself with fools, you will be foolish. If you find yourself around people who do not follow Jesus, you will be tempted to pull away as well. This is why the apostle Paul wrote, "Bad company corrupts good character" (1 Cor. 15:33).

I once heard a preacher say, "Show me your friends and I will show you your future." There is a lot of truth and wisdom in that statement. Remember the research study? Science proved that risky behaviors increased in the mere presence of peers. Now imagine those peers actually pressuring you to do something. Imagine the power of words, combined with the power of presence, coming from a peer. That is a potent influencing force. Richard Rohr is credited with saying, "You are the average sum of the five people you spend the most time with." That makes sense. Five people whom you are around often and who speak to you regularly will influence you dramatically. Whom you surround yourself with is of infinite importance and we must not take for granted. Either the company of your friends will create a character like Christ or it will corrupt your character to resemble the bad company you are friends with.

If people have such a profound influence on us, and we have a profound influence on other people, how do we determine who is a good influence? How do we determine if we are a good influence? To boil it down further, how do we determine who is a good friend? The Bible gives us that answer. I bet you did not see that coming!

God chose to tell us who the Batman is to our Robin. Our Creator tells us who us who the Timon is to our Pumbaa. The Bible tells us who a good friend is, and when we know that, we know what we ought to be to others and we know what others ought to be to us.

A Good Friend

Within the book of Proverbs, at least three characteristics of a good friend emerge. One preacher outlined part of his message on friendship with the words *shares*, *sharpens*, and *sticks*.[3] I will use the last two words, but will add a third word at the end. These three words are not the sole defining characteristics of friendship, but are the primary marks to look for in both yourself and in others. Friendship is a two-way street, and we must seek to emulate these characteristics in order to identify and relate with those who are good friends.

A Sharp Friend

Adrian Rogers said, "A true friendship will put an edge on your life." I like that. A good friend is someone who should sharpen you. The first mark of a good friend comes from Proverbs 27:17: "As iron sharpens iron, so one person sharpens another." The principle is true; people influence other people. Science proves it. The Scriptures proclaim it. Either people will sharpen you, or they will cause your life and soul to dull into ineffectiveness.

We must ask ourselves soul searching questions regarding our friendships:

1. Are my friends blunting my intelligence and my influence?
2. Are my friends damaging my character and my witness for Christ?
3. Are my friends on a trajectory course with my soul that could influence my faith, my family, my schoolwork, my relationships, and my health in an ungodly way?

A bad friend drags you down from the destiny God has in mind for you. A bad friend delays your destiny, confuses your convictions, and fumbles your faithfulness to God. "Bad company corrupts good character" said the apostle Paul (1 Cor. 15:33). If your friends facilitate sin in your life, cut them out. You can end friendships with civility and love. The other person may not respond in love, but it is better to have ended a bad friendship than to destroy your faithfulness to God.

Take an inventory of the friends you have and ask yourself, "Are they sharpening my life?" Then, ask yourself the question, "Am I sharpening them?" Do you walk away from your friendships thinking, "Wow, I am so glad that I know them"? Do you walk away and your character looks more like Christ, and their character looks more like Jesus? If not, perhaps you need to ask the question, why not?

My wife and I used to watch a particular show on Netflix. It was very popular with the younger generation and has since become a bit old, but Hannah and I used to watch it like many other people. We watched the first season, but something did not feel right. We finished the first season, each of us thinking separately about our experience. When discussing our decision to continue into the second season or not, an interesting revelation occurred. My wife and I both articulated a certain feeling of "dullness" after watching the show. We felt dull to blatant sin, evil, and immorality exemplified in the show. In fact, my wife had nightmares after watching this show. I often finished an episode thinking, "Well that was a little disgusting and disturbing." We were not being sharpened at all.

If a produced television series can create those effects on our heart, mind, and soul, imagine the profound effect friendships have on us as well? Friendships will either dull or sharpen you. I hope you choose the latter. I would prefer for you to "live with an edge on your life" that is produced by your friends. I would prefer for you to find a friend and be the friend that makes other people better. Find those people and be that person who makes other people look like, act like, and talk like Jesus.

A Sticky Friend

Not only should you want a sharp friend, but also a sticky friend. In fact, you yourself are called to be a sticky friend by God. No, I am not talking about refusing to wash your hands. A true friend is someone who remains steadfast, who sticks around and stays around. The book of Proverbs comments on this, saying, "A friend loves at all times and a brother is born for adversity" (Prov. 17:17).

A friend loves at all times. A friend sticks around at all times. In the good, and in the bad. Whether the plane is taking off or plummeting to the ground. Whether the ship sets sail or is taking on water. The people who stay around during every season of life and in the midst of your trials, temptations, mistakes, and victories are true friends.

If you want to see who your true friends are, just wait until you make a mistake. Then you will see who sticks around and who jumps ship. I experienced the brunt of this truth many years ago. I made some mistakes. I hurt some friendships. Through my sinful actions, I discovered who my real friends were. Only a select group of people stuck by me then, and I cherish those friendships still today.

Sometimes as Christians, we struggle with the word "all" and instead prefer "sometimes." We prefer to love our friends sometimes—unless they prove unworthy of our love. We consider friendships beneficial—unless someone really messes up. I often wonder if the gospel of Jesus Christ is glorified when we separate from people. I am not saying that there are not moments when separation is wise; the Scriptures indicate that there are appropriate moments of separation. Wisdom dictates appropriate moments of separation. When covenants are broken or the health and well-being of others is threatened, separation is often healthy and beneficial. Decisions to separate must always be approached with wisdom and guidance from both wiser believers and the Holy Spirit, sought for in prayer.

Unfortunately, many fail to follow proper steps in discerning decisions to separate. Often, relational fissures begin and friends become no longer friends over unnecessary reasons. Is distance from a friend wise when mistakes were made but reparations have not been exhaustively attempted?

To separate from a friend because they succumbed to sin—is that beneficial? If Jesus does not do that for the flock, for us, we must reexamine ourselves in light of His example. We must ask the question, "When my friends reveal themselves as lost and wandering sheep, do I pursue them like Jesus pursues me? Do I pursue them like a shepherd leaving his flock of ninety-nine and searching after the lost, lonely, and vulnerable one? Do I stick around when they prove they need someone to stay around and help them in the midst of their trial?"

A Friend That Stabs

I am not sure where I went wrong. First, I was teaching Nora how to help me unload and load the dishwasher. The next minute, she was running at her mother, my wife, screaming with knife in hand. Hannah cried out, "Baby with a knife!" She wasn't terrified or threatened by this tiny person. Our baby girl was eighteen months old, and I am pretty sure there was no malicious intent. At least the police report did not find any. Kidding.

So, what happened next? I ran up behind her and swiftly swiped the knife from her hand. People are not supposed to stab one another. It is not the will of God. However, it is the will of God for a good friend to "stab" another good friend. Now, you might hear that and think, "Well Derek, I don't want to be stabbed." Neither do I, not with a sharp metal object. However, a good friend is willing to pierce, cut, and pry away that which is not beneficial to his or her friend.

The third characteristic of a good friend is a willingness to stab you with truth in love. Listen to the NIV translation of Proverbs 27:6: "Wounds from a friend can be trusted, but an enemy multiplies kisses." It seems strange hearing the words "Wounds from a friend can be trusted," but notice the contrast. An enemy multiplies love and affection toward you because of an ulterior motive. An enemy will lie to your face and sing your praises while holding a knife behind their back. A friend, on the other hand, knows that truth in love is the most loving sign of affection. A friend who really loves you, who actually sticks with you through thick and thin, is not afraid to tell you the truth even if it hurts. A good friend will not give you hypocritical kisses and sing your praises regardless of your actions or words. He will do some spiritual surgery if needed. He will warn you if you are heading down a dark road. He will tell you the truth that you need to hear because the truth is the most loving thing to hear and know. He will also tell you the truth in love, because truth without love is the most unloving thing you can share. John Stott said, "Truth without love is too hard; love without truth is too soft." Warren Wiersbe wrote, "Truth without love is brutality, and love without truth is hypocrisy." A good friend avoids brutality or hypocrisy and wounds a friend with the double-edged sword of loving truth.

Many years ago I had a good friend confront me. I was in need of some spiritual surgery. With both love and truth, he administered that double-edged sword to my soul. It hurt, trust me. However, it only hurt because my life was lacking the loving truth of God. My wounds were mere flesh wounds, where my sinful pride was damaged. However, my spirit received that life-giving lesson and it stuck with me over the years.

Some time ago, it was brought to my attention that a friend of mine needed confronting. It was a hard conversation, but I was the one that needed to have it due to the circumstances of the matter. I prayed a lot before making that phone call. When God connected our cell service, my friend listened, and we are still friends today. He even thanked me for making the call, because he knew it was out of love for him that I shared the truth. It was something that needed to be shared.

The story gets better. The friend who confronted me now works side by side with the friend I called to confront. True story. Only God could orchestrate that amazing circle of truth in love. A good friend is someone who is willing to wound you with truth in love. A true friend cares enough to stab you if necessary.

The Greatest Friend

My hope for you is that you will find a good friend. If you already have one or two, I pray you will be the friend they need: a friend who sharpens, sticks, and stabs when necessary. Though that is what a good friend looks like, there is a greater friend that we all need.

In John 15, Jesus is sitting with His disciples eating a meal. It is the evening of His impending betrayal, where Judas will show his true colors as an enemy instead of a friend.

That is why Jesus is only sitting with eleven of His disciples, His friends. Judas has already left the building. He has gone to the religious leaders of the day in order to inform them of Jesus's whereabouts that night. This information will lead to Jesus's eventual arrest, trial, torture, and death by crucifixion. Judas will hand the life of an innocent man, the Son of God, over to executioners for only thirty pieces of silver.

As Judas is away, betraying his friend, Jesus is giving His true friends a directive. He says, "This is my commandment, that you love one another as I have loved you" (John 15:12). Now, up until this point, Jesus has loved them but has been alive while doing so. He is about to be betrayed by His own friend and disciple Judas. He is on the verge of being stripped naked, mocked, whipped, and enduring a crown of thorns pressed onto His head. With this impending death on the horizon, Jesus turns to his disciples, saying, "Greater love has no one than this, that someone lay down his life for his friends" (John 15:13). Jesus is about lay down His life, and He articulates that it is the ultimate expression of love. Though the sacrifices of lives to save the lives of others are always noble and moving, they pale in comparison to Jesus's sacrifice.

Jesus is about lay down His life as a sin sacrifice for the sins of the world; for us, for his disciples, and for all who would believe in Him as the greatest expression of love known to mankind. Jesus is and was the greatest friend. He surrounded himself with sinners, calling them friends (Matthew 11:19) and eating meals with them (Luke 15:1-2). He expressed the ultimate sacrifice by offering His life as a sin substitute so that we might be reconciled to God. We can only be called a friend of God because of our faith in Jesus Christ. The greatest friend to us reconciled friendship to God for us. In addition to that sacrifice and reconciliation, Jesus is the greatest friend because He always sharpens us, sticks with us, and stabs us when necessary.

When you spend time with your greatest friend, you become better for it. The Son of God puts an edge on your life. Jesus said, "Everyone then who hears these words of mine and does them will be like a wise man who built his house on the rock" (Matt. 7:24). When you build your life on the Son of God, you become wise. Jesus is the source of all wisdom, because Jesus is God in the flesh. Any time spent learning about, listening to, and obeying our Lord will sharpen your life, for both this world and the world to come.

Jesus is also the greatest friend because He always sticks around. If you have trusted Jesus as your Lord and Savior, and believed in your heart that God raised him from the dead, you will be saved (Romans 10:9). Listen to what Romans also says for believers of the resurrection: "For I am convinced that neither death nor life, neither angels nor demons, neither the present nor the future, nor any powers, neither height nor depth, nor anything else in all creation, will be able to separate us from the love of God that is in Christ Jesus our Lord" (8:38-39). Nothing will separate you from the love of Christ. That is to say, Jesus sticks around through the good and bad. That is a good friend.

Jesus is the greatest friend because He stabs you when necessary. Do you know the first sermon Jesus preached? He spoke these words: "Repent, for the kingdom of heaven is near" (Matt. 4:17). The Son of God is not afraid to do spiritual surgery. That was the meaning of his mission. He came to heal the sick and call sinners to salvation, because all have sinned and fallen short of the glory of God. Jesus came, with the sword of truth embodied in His life and words, to convict the world of sin. Jesus came to cauterize our wounded hearts and remove the infection of sin that sickens us. Jesus is our greatest friend.

A New Way

My desire for you is to pave a new way forward in your friendships. Perhaps you have made some mistakes in choosing your friends. Ok, you can start over today. Perhaps you have failed miserably in the area of being a good friend. This too, can end today. God desires for you to not only find good friends but also to be a good friend. There is great power in friendship.

There is no way to state the importance of friendship other than saying, "People influence you and you influence other people." With that in mind, the power lies in our hearts and hands. There is power in our words, our actions, and our relationships. Will we use that power to pave a way forward that brings honor and glory to God? Will we pave a way forward that sees our friendships influencing one another to run hard after Jesus? People will either influence for bad or for good. Jesus's life influenced people. He is the greatest friend. Now, it is our calling to first believe in and know our greatest friend, Jesus Christ, so we can then be a great friend to others in His name and for His name.

Talk About It

1. Have you ever been influenced by someone to do something you would later regret?
2. Proverbs 13:20 says, "Whoever walks with the wise becomes wise, but the companion of fools will suffer harm." Describe some of the positive and negative outcomes of friendships that you have witnessed, either in your life or the lives of others.
3. The Bible says that that bad company corrupts good character (1 Corinthians 15:33). How have you seen this truth play out in your life or the lives of others?

4. Read Matthew 18:15-20. How do these verses apply to friendships? How would your friendships benefit from having these principles applied to them?
5. Describe how Jesus fulfills every aspect of a good friend.
6. In what ways do you emulate Jesus Christ in your friendships? In what ways do you see room for improvement? What is your next step toward improving your friendships?

Do It

1. Many people have said, "Show me your friends and I will show you your future." Take an inventory of your friendships and write down the future you see with them in your life. Pray about that future, asking God to give you clarity about pursuing or removing those friendships.
2. After praying, challenge your friends to read this chapter together and then talk about it afterward.

FAMILY FEUD

It was January 15, 1944. The story goes that an aviation cadet strolled out to his airplane for a solo practice flight.[4] After checking the plane's instruments and clearing his takeoff, the cadet signaled a farewell message to the control tower. Soon, both pilot and plane were no longer in sight. Moments after takeoff, the cadet's vision became blurry, and then his eyesight turned black.

Unexpectedly stricken blind, the pilot radioed a panicked message back to the control tower. Hearing this unusual cry for help, the control officer responded over the pilot's radio, "Follow my instructions implicitly." The tower officer began issuing a series of commands including keeping the blinded cadet circling above the landing field. The entire runway was cleared, and an ambulance arrived on the scene. As the pilot circled, the control officer's voice crackled over the radio, "Now lose altitude." The pilot began to descend from his lofty holding pattern. Again, the blind pilot heard the control tower, "Now bank sharply." The airplane banked suddenly until the pilot heard the words, "You're coming onto the field now." Blind, but following the tower officer's instructions, the pilot brought the plane to a perfect landing. The cadet's life was saved, and later, his sight was restored.

Remind me to never fly in an airplane with that guy. The life of a man, flying blind, hung in the balance with the words, "Follow my instructions implicitly." When it comes to the family, I believe many teenagers today are like that young cadet. Just as students begin to take off, venture on their own, and attempt to pilot their airplane called family, they begin to lose sight of how to successfully navigate it. I believe God is in the control tower, clearly speaking over the microphone, saying, "Follow my instructions implicitly."

When we follow instructions, life goes well. Take a plane for example: When you follow instructions concerning how to properly fly an aircraft, you will remain safe and alive. However, when you fail to follow instructions, your life is at risk, and the lives of others in the plane with you. If you found yourself skydiving, you would want to follow instructions so that life goes well, and keeps going well as you safely land on the ground. Failing to follow instructions will complicate and possibly even shorten your life.

My desire for you is to live a good, long, and holy life. In regards to the family, I hope for you to successfully navigate your role within the family and not crash and burn. The only way to do that is to follow the instructions of God implicitly. However, the reality is that many students are stricken with blindness in regards to their families. Many students are blind to the blessing that family is.

Flying Blind in the Family

There are at least two reasons why many students are blind to the blessing their family is. The first reason is a failure to remember that their family is a blessing given to them by God. This foundational light bulb of truth begins to flicker in the teenage years. A teenager might articulate that families are blessings and gifts from God, but many struggle to believe their own family is heaven sent. Yet, James 1:17 clearly articulates that "every good gift and every perfect gift is from above." This includes the family, both yours and mine. God invented the family, and to say it is not a gift is to call His creative genius and good nature into question.

I like to think of it in terms of the show Shark Tank. Behind one sixty-minute segment are many creative and talented minds that come together to make the show happen. Directors, producers, entrepreneurs, scouts—not to mention a host of behind-the-scenes crew, marketers, and administrative support.

When it comes to the family, God is director, producer, entrepreneur, inventor, and behind-the-scenes support. He invented the family like an entrepreneur, and then mass produced it like a shark could. In Ephesians 3, the apostle Paul says, "For this reason I bow my knees before the Father, from whom every family in heaven and on earth is named" (Eph. 3:14-15). Did you catch what Paul is saying? He articulates that God named his invention. God named the family, and created it (James 1:17).

As we have already learned concerning sex, the family is also a good gift from a good God. Your family is a gift from God to you and for you, but many students struggle to believe that. Many students do not believe their family is either a gift or a blessing. Much of this struggle finds its origin in sin and in raging against the divine authority structure put in place since creation. Parent are entrusted with heaven granted responsibility to care, provide, and train children or students in the way they should go (Proverbs 22:6). It is this blindness to the goodness of the family, originating from a good God, that causes turbulence in many students' lives.

The second reason many teenagers are blind to the blessing of family is that many students are blind to the truth that every family is fallen from God. There is a profound disconnect in many students' theologies from the fact that they and their families are imperfect sinners in need of saving grace. Instead, idealistic pedestal models of perfect parents, siblings, and family dynamics cloud the mind of reason for many teens today.

I remember experiencing this blindness myself. When I began noticing character flaws in others, the spotlight often hovered over my family. However, the Scriptures are clear in reminding us that every family is sinful, imperfect, and falls short of the glory of God (Romans 3:23). In fact, the very first family, that of Adam and Eve, set the entire world into motion and created the sinful environment we are born into, the sinful body we are born with, and the sinful spirit we inherit. Furthermore, Adam and Eve's son, Cain, murdered his brother Abel because of jealousy and anger. That is a lot of baggage—and both major events occur within the first four chapters of the first book of the Bible.

Before we even leave Genesis, the family drama intensifies. Sin is on flagrant display. Sarah grieves her infertility, so she gives Hagar to Abraham. Her maid servant is to bear a surrogate child. When the plan is successful, Sarah becomes angry and jealous, abusing Hagar. When Sarah's natural born son Isaac matures, he marries Rebekah. They give birth to two twin boys, and each parent has a favorite child. A house divided leads to one of the worst sibling rivalries in all of history (Genesis 25). Again, that is all in the first book of the Bible. Families are sinful, messy, and dysfunctional. We could continue this observational lesson to include Jacob's twelve sons, David's dysfunctional family, and Solomon's wise beginning but unwise ending, which led to a split kingdom.

I think you get the point. No one is perfect and no family is without sin. Every family has issues. We are all sinners needing saving grace. Each and every relative of ours who bears the same last name, or another name, needs the one whose name is above every other name, Jesus. Every family has sin and needs saving. Your own awkward one and your neighborhood friends' as well.

No family is perfect, because every family is fallen from God. But just because a family has sin does not mean it is not still a blessing from God. This failure to see our families as blessings from God, but also fallen from God, is the blindness that inhibits many of us from safely landing and thriving in our God-given roles within our families.

So how should we view our role in the family? How do we safely land the plane in order to both survive and thrive within the family? We must obey instructions from the control tower implicitly. If we do, we will not crash and burn while navigating the family. If we do not, the consequences will be devastating. We find our instructions within the Word of God. Primarily, we discover two instructions that bring about a safe landing. We find two requirements that result in a reward. Obedience to these requirements will bring about a reward, and that reward will be long life within the family.

Obey Your Parents

The first instruction for safely navigating the family originates in Ephesians 6:1: "Children, obey your parents in the Lord, for this is right." It is the will of God for children to obey their parents. This is the first instruction from the control tower in order to safely navigate the family. The radio crackles to life for us with a proper order of life. Children obey parents; parents instruct, lead, and guide children. That order is paramount, as the word *obey* conveys the idea of complying with someone else's command, direction, or request—that is, obedience means submitting to the authority of another. Children submit to their parents' authority. Children follow and comply with the commands and direction of their parents.

This is not an uncommon notion, as children are naturally geared this way. With stern but loving corrections, children are wired to listen to their parents. There is a natural order to the relationship that fosters this submission. That is what the apostle Paul appeals to here in Ephesians—a circle of life. A child is the product of parents. Therefore, a child is wired from birth for dependence on his or her parents. From the womb, each child was born completely incapable of surviving on its own. As a child naturally develops, parents will teach children how to survive and thrive in the world. There is a daily exchange of survival techniques, knowledge, and wisdom that will aid in the growth of the child. Naturally, the older and wiser teach the younger and simpler. Teachers have students, and parents have children. The child learns or obeys the teachings and authority of the parent. There is a right and natural order to the relationship between parent and child. The nature of the family is to nurture a loving and submissive family order.

I love puppies. (How is that for a transition sentence?) My mother-in-law recently acquired a newborn pup. I was in love. It is amazing how you forget the restless nights of potty training and furniture replacement when you see the tiny versions of your animals. It is like God intentionally made them cute so you could endure the frustrations associated with cuteness. I have determined that the cuter something is, the more expensive, attentive, and potentially spoiled it will be.

Anyway, puppies love to bite when they play. It is the only aspect of puppies I do not like. The only way they will know whether their bite is too hard is if someone tells them. It is often the mother dog that tells them if they are biting too hard. When an excited puppy bites too hard during playtime, mom will give a loud yelp in order to startle the pup. If the puppy bites again, mom may even growl and show teeth. If the puppy bites a third time, mom may even bite back.

A mother dog teaches her puppy how to play nicely. It is ingrained in its nature. It is also ingrained in the nature of your parents. There is an order to nature: the younger learn from the older. I could not tell you how many times my wife and I say "No" or "No ma'am" to Nora. Now that I think about it, the word *no* prefaces our daughter's name. Foreshadowing much? We tell our daughter no on a daily basis. In fact, we tell her no to the same things on a daily basis. She attempts to throw things away that she should not. I have a feeling we have thrown away some pretty valuable and useful things. Good thing our treasure is in heaven. However, whenever Nora attempts to do something that is not right for her, we correct her. That correction is not always met with approval from her end, but she recognizes our authority and will usually cease and desist. It is ingrained in her to obey us, and it is sin that causes her to disobey us at times.

Now, it is beneficial for us to briefly mention that there are times when parents are not being good parents. There are times when parents will tell you to do things that are not honoring to God and that are not for your good. This is the exception, not the norm, but at times parents will severely hurt and abuse their children. If you are reading this, and this describes you, please know there is a safe place for you to talk about that. As I mentioned before, my web address is located at the back of this book and I would be happy to both hear you out and point you in the direction of help, hope, and healing. Again, we need to stress, this is the exception and not the norm.

What I have found in the majority of issues that students articulate regarding their parents is a desire to rid themselves of this commandment from God. They desire to buck the system of nature and free themselves from the instruction or the right order of listening to and obeying one's parents. They forget or reject Colossians 3:20: "Children, obey your parents in everything, for this pleases the Lord." They forget that they are under this obligation until they are no longer children. When they are taking care of themselves, and possibly even starting their own family through marriage, they are no longer required to follow this instruction. However, unless they are adults, capable of providing for their own needs and the needs of a family, the first instruction from the control tower regarding their family is obedience. Obedience brings blessing. Any and every student who obeys their parents will safely navigate the runway and land their plane. This is pleasing to the Lord and the natural way of life.

Honor Your Parents

The second instruction for a safe landing in the family is for children to honor their parents. This instruction is explicit from the control tower as the apostle Paul continues communicating to children, saying, "'Honor your father and mother' (this is the first commandment with a promise)" (Eph. 6:2). First, children are to obey. Second, honor is to exist within the parent-child relationship.

We find the first mention of this instruction in Exodus 20. In fact, it is the very text that Paul quotes while writing to the Ephesian church. In other words, he says remember your fore-fathers who received the law from Moses; remember the people of Israel who received those first ten commandments. One of those commandments instructed them to honor their fathers and mothers. This command to remember the Old Testament law is not abnormal; in fact, every one of the Ten Commandments is affirmed or strengthened in the New Testament except for the command to remember the Sabbath.

It is the fifth commandment, to honor one's parents, that Paul cites here as the second instruction for landing safely within the family. Teenagers and children are to not only obey, but also to honor their parents. *Obedience* connotes the idea of exter-nal action. It is complying to a command or request. However, *honor* conveys the idea of internal respect, love, and adoration. Honoring someone is showing care through both your actions and your attitude. That is to say, not only does God care about obeying parents regardless of attitude; He also cares about the attitude behind your actions. It is this holistic love toward oth-ers— the second greatest commandment according to Jesus (Mark 12:31)—in both attitudes and actions that reflects the will of God. This is the control tower of Scripture commanding chil-dren to land safely with both obedience and honor.

The Scriptures are rife with commands to honor others. Romans 13:7 says, "Pay to all what is owed to them: taxes to whom taxes are owed, revenue to whom revenue is owed, respect to whom respect is owed, honor to whom honor is due." When we fail to honor others, it shows foolishness on our parts and brings dishonor to our parents. Listen to how Proverbs puts it: "A wise son makes a glad father, but a foolish son is a sorrow to his mother" (Prov. 10:1). Dishonoring your parents is unwise, disrespectful, and unloving. It is a foolish way of living and brings pain and sorrow to your life, to your relationship with your parents, and to their relationship with you.

There was a time in my life when I was blind to the blessing of my family. There was also a time in my life when I was blind to the imperfections of my family. I remember a season of life where I struggled to treat my family with honor and respect. I obeyed them, for the most part, but the attitude behind my actions told another story. I was rude at times. I was disrespectful. I would push against boundaries and it affected my relationship with them. Looking back, I pray that my own daughter and future children will successfully navigate the murky waters of sin and wade out of the pool of disobedience into the lovely waters of blessing. I am blessed to have my family, and I am thankful that they continued to love me through my lack of love, honor, and respect to them within my mechanical obedience.

Family members who honor one another; children listening to parents in obedience with respect, love, and admiration: it is they who are blessed. Proverbs 8:32 says, "And now, O sons, listen to me: blessed are those who keep my ways." This is the way of wisdom talking, as a parent to a son. This is the way of honor and obedience, paving the road of blessing for your life. I love how Proverbs describes a godly woman whose children "rise and call her blessed" (31:28). I can only imagine that this blessing derives from children who heeded a godly woman's teaching. This mother taught her children both obedience and honor, and they were blessed for heeding it. Now, they return the blessing of a loving relationship to their mother by calling her blessed, and by practicing the honor, respect, and love that was both taught to them and caught by them.

A Promise

Are you familiar with the "Life is Good" company? Their tagline is "Spread the power of optimism," and it has made them a lot of money. They even donate ten percent of their net profits to help kids in need. My wife really loves their stores and clothing, and it makes me smile. I enjoy her pleasure in perusing these retail outlets because it is a beautiful representation of her inner character. She has a way of looking at the bright side of life, with an ever-present dose of reality as well. When life gives her lemons, she makes lemonade. When the lemons go bad or the store runs out, she looks for limes instead. She refuses to sit around and say, "Woe is me," or boycott the store for its failure to supply her demand.

The second instruction to children regarding honoring their parents carries a hint of optimism in it. Listen again to the instruction: "'Honor your father and mother' (this is the first commandment with a promise)" (Eph. 6:2). This is to say that when you obey and honor your parents, a promise exists for you. This is the first and only of the Ten Commandments that carries a promise with it in the New Testament. What is that promise? Ephesians 6:3 says, "That it may go well with you and that you may live long in the land." In other words, life is good. Life is good when life is going well and when you live long in the land.

Funerals are especially difficult when a family member passes away. However, when that family member has lived a long and good life, what is often said? "He lived a long, good life," or "She lived life to the full." Sometimes we may even use words such as, "At her age it was expected." Tragic funerals are those of men, women, or even children who lived a short life on this earth. The promise given to children who obey and honor their parents is a promise of blessing. Warren Wiersbe identified two blessings for children who obeyed the control tower of Scripture regarding their family: "Life will be good and life will be long." Obedience does not guarantee a life free from trials or even a long life, but it will greatly increase the pleasure, purpose, and longevity of your life. Danger always exists when we disobey our parents. Danger always exists when we refuse to listen to the control tower. Satan and your sin seeks to steal, kill, and destroy, but "Life is Good" for the student who navigates his family well, who listens to the control tower. Obedience always brings blessing.

This is my charge to teenagers today: listen to the control tower. We are all blinded by sin, but if we follow His instructions implicitly, God will help us to navigate the family. Obedience to God is first and foremost, because it then directs and governs our obedience to our parents. In fact, when we obey our earthly parents, it evidences our obedience to our heavenly Father. Children are called to submit to their parents. It is the right order of life. It is the right way of living. When this order exists in our families, we see the fruit of our faith. We see planes safely navigating the trials and difficulties of the family.

Jesus, Obey Your Parents!

Sometimes we need a little encouragement to do something. We often need a model, or a mentor, to aid us in doing something we ought to do or to teach us something we should know. When I think of obeying parents, Jesus comes to mind. I know, I know, this is the perfect Sunday school answer, am I right? However, think about the reality of Jesus's birth and the resulting obedience that it demanded. When the Word became flesh, the Son of God also became the son of Mary and Joseph. Now Jesus had three parents to submit to. Jesus listened to and obeyed God the Father, plus an earthly mother and father. With each parent came the same demand of obedience to them.

In Luke 2, Mary and Joseph found Jesus in the temple. On their return home from Jerusalem after celebrating the Passover, they realized their son was missing. A frantic search ensued for their missing boy, ending in the culminating discovery that Jesus was still in Jerusalem at the temple. The Bible records Mary's exasperated declaration: "Son, why have you treated us so? Behold, your father and I have been searching for you in great distress" (Luke 2:48). His response was confusing to them, but not to us.

"Why were you looking for me? Did you not know that I must be in my Father's house?" (2:49). At a young age, Jesus revealed an awareness of multiple parents. His obedience was to both a heavenly father and earthly parents. The next verse reveals a life of obedience to Mary and Joseph, as "he went down with them and came to Nazareth and was submissive to them. And his mother treasured up all these things in her heart" (2:51). The New International Version uses the word "obedient" instead of submissive. Both versions convey the same idea. Jesus was obedient to Mary and Joseph.

Furthermore, Jesus was also obedient to a heavenly Father. His will was subsumed by the will of God. Jesus said, "By myself I can do nothing; I judge only as I hear, and my judgment is just, for I seek not to please myself but him who sent me" (John 5:30). Self-seeking will was not present in Christ our Lord. Even in His words, Jesus revealed a God-ordained speech pattern, "For I did not speak on my own, but the Father who sent me commanded me to say all that I have spoken" (John 12:49). The Savior was obedient in will and obedient in word.

The difference between the obedience of Christ and our own obedience is the reality of sin. We are sinners who fall short of the glory of God (Romans 3:23). Jesus Christ never sinned. Hebrews declares that our high priest Jesus can empathize with our weakness to sin because he was tempted in the same ways we are (4:15). However, the difference between Christ and us is His consistent obedience to the law of God. The author of Hebrews says that our high priest was tempted, for certain, but He "did not sin" for certain. Even Jesus said, "Can any of you prove me guilty of sin? If I am telling the truth, why don't you believe me?" (John 8:46). The only consistency regarding our obedience to the law is our inconsistency. All have sinned and fallen short of the glory of God. All, that is, except Jesus Christ.

Our propensity to sin, and that universal condition of every man, woman, and child to sin, began in the garden of Eden. Adam and Eve, tempted by Satan, disobeyed the law of God and plunged the world into sin. Adam, being the head representative of mankind, carries the weight of that responsibility. The Bible names him as the main transmitter, saying, "For as by the one man's disobedience the many were made sinners..." (Romans 5:19). This was not to relieve Eve of her guilt, but simply to become a parallel beacon of hope for the good news that was to come. The bad news is that sin came by the one man's disobedience, allowing his family to fall into sin. The good news is found in the obedience of Jesus Christ. The good news is found in the one man who brought about justice, forgiveness, and righteousness through His obedience. This is the great reversal.

Romans 5:19 continues, "...so by the one man's obedience the many will be made righteous." Our disobedience, beginning in the garden, brought upon the sinful plight we find ourselves in: separated from God, dead in our trespasses, and headed for an eternity in hell. Pain, punishment, and torture await us. However, the good news is that the obedience of one man, Jesus Christ, will be the escape ladder for many, otherwise destined to burn in the flames of hell brought about by their sin. We who believe in Jesus Christ will be made righteous by the obedience of the Savior.

The apostle Paul articulates how Jesus, in human form, expressed obedience to God by fulfilling the plan of heaven through dying on a cross (Philippians 2:8). This death, of an innocent man, would satisfy the wrath of God toward sinners. The just punishment of our sins would be paid by another, Jesus Christ, who knew no sin. 2 Corinthians 5:21 states, "For our sake he made him to be sin who knew no sin, so that in him we might become the righteousness of God." It was the loving will of God the Father, expressed by the obedient love of God the Son, that put Jesus on the cross to die the for the sins of the world. For God so loved the world that Jesus was sent for those who would believe in Him as their sin substitute (John 3:16). Those who would believe in Jesus Christ as their Lord and Savior would be forgiven their sins, welcomed into the family of God, and guaranteed a future with God in heaven. The sinless sacrifice, obedient unto death, obedient to both earthly and heavenly parents, is our model and example of obedience on earth. If Jesus could obey God unto death, and obey His parents without sin, we can certainly strive to obey our parents. We may not do so perfectly, but we can strive to do so with the utmost love, honor, and respect because He paid it all in obedience for us. In turn, we can obey our heavenly Father and our earthly parents.

Talk About It

1. Do you sometimes struggle to believe or articulate that your family is a blessing from God? Why or why not?
2. Do you struggle to believe the truth that every family is fallen and in need of salvation? Do you struggle to believe that every family member is a sinner, in need of salvation?
3. On a scale of one to ten, where do you land in regards to obeying your parents? If this question is not applicable, where would you say your children land?
4. When do the limitations of obeying one's parents shift?
5. On a scale of one to ten, where do you land in regards to honoring your parents? If this question is not applicable, where would you say your children land?
6. How does the obedience of Jesus Christ model obedience for us in our homes?

7. In what specific ways do you struggle to both honor and obey your parents? If this question is not applicable, where would you say your children could improve?

Do It

For Teenagers: Spend some time thinking about how you can practically show love, honor and obedience to your parents. Write out your next step. Also, write out your fears, and bring them before the Lord in prayer.

For Parents or Small Group Leaders: Spend some time praying for your child or small group to love, honor, and obey you or their parents. Think about how you can practically teach, model, and train your child or group to love, honor, and obey you as parents, or to obey their parents.

FINANCIAL FORTITUDE

Christmas is my favorite holiday—the most wonderful time of year. As soon as the seasonal music begins playing on the radio, the station hardly changes in my car. Festive lights adorn many houses, most noticeably at night. Nora sits in the back of our car ogling over the lights, pointing and exclaiming, "Lights! Lights!"

It is the only time of year when we eat dinner at a friend's home and then watch a Christmas movie on a Monday evening. No other time of year would you do that. That may become a new tradition. Speaking of traditions, Hannah and I have begun another new tradition: We each created our lists. Now, these are no crayon-and-notepad lists. These are the technologically savvy, culturally cool Amazon Wish Lists. The downside to our lists is that you need wi-fi and electricity. Pencil and paper for the win again! It is amazing where we have come as a culture though. I remember my mother asking me to write out a wish list for Christmas. Giving me that blank piece of paper had an amazing way of raising my hopes. My parents also had an amazing way of making that list disappear at Christmas to prevent me from cross-checking my gifts with my list. Smart. Taking a note out of their book.

It is interesting how age and experience change the Christmas experience. By the time I graduated into high school, the wish list experience had faded into memory. The one thing I asked for was the universal request of almost every single high school student.

"Derek, what do you want for Christmas?"

Cue the Christmas song, "All I want for Christmas is.... cold, hard, cash." I remember sharing this talk at high school TRIB3. In response to my inquiry regarding what every high school student wants for Christmas, there was a resounding chorus of, "Money." Why do we all crave the same thing at the same age? Why do we no longer desire physical gifts but only desire the means to purchase said gifts? I believe the answer to that question lies in a God-given desire for the freedom and responsibility behind the cash. That is, I believe the yearning for personal responsibility and decision making regarding our finances is an outward expression of the God-given desire imprinted on our souls.

Stewards of Saving and Spending

God created us to be stewards of creation. That is, we were created to manage and look after what ultimately belongs to God. It is the role that was given to Adam and Eve, and it encompassed the responsibilities of tending the garden of Eden, ruling over both the animal and plant kingdoms, and multiplying the existence of man to fulfill their God-given duties. It is a divinely created job description that extends even into our finances. We are commanded to steward our finances for the glory of God. We are commanded to steward both our saving and our spending.

When I was young, my parents purchased four miniature coin banks. If I remember correctly, those small circular banks represented various sports. One bank, shaped like a golf ball, was for tithing my money back to God. Another bank, the soccer ball, was designated for savings. The tennis ball bank was called "caring" and was aptly described as the bank we used to buy gifts for people. Finally, my favorite bank, was called "spending," and it was shaped like a baseball. For some reason, that bank seemed to glow a bit. I often felt like Indiana Jones staring down a hidden artifact when I looked at that bank.

Now, why would a grown man and woman take money out of their own pockets to buy four banks? Furthermore, why would my parents not only spend money on those four banks, but then spend more money by dividing it up between the four banks in order to teach me a lesson? That object lesson was rooted in the fundamental conviction that God has designed our souls to "steward" our finances. My parents felt compelled to answer the question that I was not even asking yet: "How should I handle my finances?" They desired to instill in me an understanding that we have both the freedom and responsibility to use money. However, the answer is a bit a more complicated than simply freedom and responsibility. My parents yearned for me to know that God's will is for us to steward our finances, instead of squandering them.

Jesus and Money

Did you know that money is one of the most talked about subjects in the Bible? In fact, there are more references to money and possessions in the Bible than passages concerning prayer and faith combined. Of all the subjects Jesus talked about, money was one of the most significant. About forty-two percent of Jesus's parables were concerned with handling money and possessions.

The Bible speaks of finances so much because God desires for us to properly steward our money instead of squandering it. Stewarding is part of the original job description given to mankind in the garden. Many teenagers today ask the question, "How should I handle my finances?" God gives a resounding, simple, and straightforward answer: steward them.

Speaking of stewards and squanderers, Jesus told a story about those very words. This one parable is part of the forty-two percent, and in it we find a steward by title but a squanderer by character. That is, we find a steward by job description, but a squanderer by daily habits. He may have talked the talk, but he did not walk the walk. God wants you to be a steward and not a squanderer.

In Luke 16:1-14, Jesus is talking to his disciples and begins telling a story about a rich man who had a manager. Accusations were brought against the wealthy man's steward (16:1). That morning, the rich man called for his breakfast, and in between bites of bagel, he requested the morning newspaper. The headlines read, "Steward or Squanderer?" naming the manager as complicit in mishandling the master's money. Checking his social media feed, the rich man also noticed a popular hashtag circulating on Twitter, saying #whereisthemoneygoing? He called his manager and said, "You're fired" (16:2).

Now, when we read the word *manager*, we could replace it with the word *steward*. A steward or manager is someone in charge of the master's estate, someone who can even act on behalf of the master. Do you remember Joseph in Genesis 39? He was a slave being traded in Egypt and was eventually purchased by Potiphar, Captain of Pharaoh's Guard. Potiphar saw the favor of God on Joseph's life and put his new slave in charge of everything he owned. Joseph became an overseer, manager, or steward of everything that his master owned. The Bible says Joseph took care of everything for his master other than deciding what his master would eat that day.

According to Jesus, the manager in the parable was in charge of his master's estate, and he was clearly complicit in the accusations brought against him. He was a squanderer, dipping into his master's money for himself. He was a squanderer, possibly spending more money than the master actually had. He was a squanderer, perhaps lazy and not putting the time into the estate that it needed, causing the business ventures to fall flat. The wicked steward acknowledges that he is "guilty as charged" because he doesn't even put up a fight. He simply accepts his fate, knowing that he is guilty, and begins to ponder his next steps in order to survive (16:3). He sits back and thinks, "What am I going to do? If I lose my job, I lose my lifestyle. I have grown quite accustomed to my new way of living. I like the camels I ride, and the fine Egyptian cotton sheets I sleep on. My wine cellar is filled with the finest and choicest selections. The refrigerator is stocked and I barely lift a finger to do anything. How can I afford to live after all of this is taken away from me?" The end is certainly near.

Just when he thinks all is lost, a metaphoric light bulb clicks above his head. A plan is hatched. The scheme is conceived. If you did not think this man was dishonest already, his ensuing plan reveals that he is. In order to ensure his future, he hatches a plan to ingratiate himself to his master's debtors. He thinks, "If I can make friends with those who owe my master money, when I lose my job, I can stay with them until I find another job—or possibly even work for them instead." So he comes up with a plan to offer large discounts to the people that owe his master money.

Calling the first debtor into his office, he says, "How much money do you owe my master?"

The man replies, "A hundred measures of oil." In an agricultural society, food, land, and livestock were popular means of payment.

The shrewd, squandering manager said, "Take the bill and cut it in half. Write fifty measures and pay up today." Talk about Black Friday savings.

The next debtor walks in after the first, and the manager says, "How much do you owe my master?"

The man holds his hat, sweaty from working the field, and says, "A hundred measures of wheat."

Squandering Steve (that's what we will call him) thinks to himself, then gives a twenty percent discount, saying "Take your bill, cut it by twenty percent, and write eighty." At some point the money is collected, friendships are formed, and the dishonest manager's boss is actually impressed with his former employee's shrewdness.

I don't think Steve's boss was impressed that he just lost thirty-five percent of the income due to him; I believe the rich man was impressed that his wicked steward had just secured his future after his firing. I think he was impressed that his former employee didn't fall flat on his face but rebounded after brief unemployment. Notice what Jesus says next: "...For the sons of this world are shrewder in dealing with their own generation than the sons of light. And I tell you, make friends for yourselves by means of unrighteous wealth, so that when it fails they may receive you into the eternal dwellings" (Luke 16:9).

Now, admittedly, this is a very confusing passage for many people. The answer is really quite simple. Jesus is simply using this story to illustrate a point: use your master's money wisely. The dishonest manager was mishandling his master's money. He was squandering what was entrusted to him. When his demise came in the end, he used his last act of managing his master's money to make friends for himself by offering discounted debt. That is to say, he made friends with his master's money. He banked on the fact that they would support him in his time of need, after he was fired.

Comparing that to us today, the lesson is similar. We must use the master's money wisely. We must ensure our future by making friends with our finances. Think of it from an eternal perspective—that is to say, we are to point people to Jesus, investing our money in sharing the good news of the gospel with others. When we fund the gospel and use our money to tell others about the life, death, and resurrection of Jesus Christ, we help bring sinners to salvation. Those saved through the gospel, and funded in part by our resources, will secure for themselves heavenly dwellings. Listen to Jesus's words in John: "Let not your hearts be troubled. Believe in God; believe also in me. In my Father's house are many rooms. If it were not so, would I have told you that I go to prepare a place for you? And if I go and prepare a place for you, I will come again and will take you to myself, that where I am you may also be" (John 14:1-3).

When we use our money to proclaim the Gospel, we make friends for eternity. Heaven waits for those of us who have believed in Jesus Christ as Lord and Savior, and friendships await in eternity in the homes of those in whom we have invested with our finances. Our own homes will also be heavenly hospitalities for those who have used their wealth to point us to the true riches of God.

A Picture of a Faithful Steward

Beginning in Luke 16:10, we find a pivot in the parable. There is a noticeable change of tone and pace when Jesus begins to describe a picture of a faithful steward. He answers the question that formulates in our mind: "What does a faithful steward look like?" Throughout the next four verses, we find three characteristics of a faithful steward.

Faithful for the Future

Luke 16:10 says, "One who is faithful in a very little is also faithful in much, and one who is dishonest in a very little is also dishonest in much." In this short sentence, Jesus reveals the first characteristic of a faithful steward. That picture includes the reality that a steward is faithful for the future while a squanderer is destructive to his destiny. That is to say, how you handle your finances today, regardless of size, has a profound impact on how you will handle your finances in the future. Hudson Taylor said, "Small things are small things but faithfulness with a small thing is a big thing." Why did my parents buy me four banks before I could even work my first job? They believed in this principle. The habits you begin today will drive you toward your destiny. Many teenagers today believe their paychecks are too small to concern themselves with budgeting or financial stewardship. The importance is not in the size but in the stewardship. How you handle the small things in life will determine how you will handle the large things of life. Learning to budget money now will impact your future for the better. Learning to freely give your money now will impact your faith for the better. If you squander your biweekly paycheck from work today, what makes you think you will not squander your bimonthly paycheck after college or when you enter the workforce? How you handle the small things of life is an indicator of how you will most likely handle the large things in life. If God sees that you cannot prove faithful with even a small amount of wealth, He may not bless you with more wealth to use for His glory when you will spend it on your own glory.

Take a look at Luke 16:11 as well: "If then you have not been faithful in the unrighteous wealth, who will entrust to you the true riches?" How you handle your finances is a direct indicator of the state of your relationship with God. The way you spend your money evidences your character, your faith, and ultimately your destiny. Ralph Waldo Emerson is attributed with this fantastic quote: "Sow a thought and you reap an action; sow an action and you reap a habit; sow a habit and you reap a character; sow a character and you reap a destiny." Apply that quote to the dishonest manager, and observe what you find. He sowed a thought of cheating his master out of his money. He then sowed the action of doing so, reaping a habit of mismanaging someone else's money. That habit of embezzling funds or spending more than the master earned led to a character of dishonesty. His dishonest character then led him to the ultimate destiny of discovered treachery, and then he was fired from his job. Ultimately, his squandering of his master's money led to a destructive destiny. A steward is faithful for the future while a squanderer is not.

One Master

Jesus said, "No servant can serve two masters, for either he will hate the one and love the other, or he will be devoted to the one and despise the other. You cannot serve God and money" (Luke 16:13). Every follower of Jesus is engaged in a battle to dethrone the alluring idol called money. A faithful steward will only serve one master. The battle strategy for this temptation is an "either-or" ultimatum from our Savior and Lord: Either you will hate money, or you will hate God; either you will love money, or you will love God. You will either devote yourself to the riches of heaven or the riches of earth. You must make the choice. There is no middle ground. There is no "no man's land" when it comes to wealth.

This posture seems harsh at first, but it comes from the lips of our Savior. We must hear the words of God in the flesh with the utmost soberness. Money has a tremendous pull on many. It promises security, comfort, prestige and power, which all feed into our sinful and selfish hearts. There is only one throne in heaven, and God sits on it. There is only one throne in our hearts, and God is to be our first love, but for many, money dethrones the Creator and plunges their souls into ruin. Hear what the Bible says: "For the love of money is a root of all kinds of evils. It is through this craving that some have wandered away from the faith and pierced themselves with many pangs" (1 Tim. 6:10). Money has the allure and temptation to cause you to wander away from faith in God, producing much pain in your life.

I think it is important for us to stop and recognize that money itself is not the temptation; the *love* of money is a root of all kinds of evils. Loving anything above God is idolatry. However, speaking of money, Jesus says it is impossible to serve both. In fact, it is dangerous to serve both God and money. When I think of dangerous, I think of the twelfth century. During this time, European Christians would engage in "holy wars" or crusades to both conquer and protect the Holy Land. Howard Dayton recounts how crusaders would hire mercenaries to fight in their stead at times. One of the requirements of these mercenaries was to undergo Christian baptism before fighting.[5] Dayton further recounts that these hired killers would wade into the water for the ritual and would hold their swords out of the water. It was as if they said, "Jesus Christ is my Lord and Savior, except for my sword and whichever way I swing it or whomever I swing it at!"

That picture is a fitting illustration for many teenagers and believers today. We profess Jesus as our Lord and Savior, and many of us are baptized. However, we never consider that our faith demands loving God over our money. Dayton describes many Christians as those who hold their wallets out of the water of faith and say, "God, you can be the Lord of my entire life except for my money. I am perfectly capable of handling that myself."[6] Many have said that, and many have wandered away from the faith. Many have said that and have pierced themselves with much pain. When you cannot wholly devote your soul to God, money will only prove a barrier to fellowship with, faith in, and faithfulness to God. You cannot serve both God and money.

Is Heaven Your Treasure?

The Gospel of Luke describes a very sobering scene. After Jesus shares the story of the unfaithful steward with His disciples, including two characteristics of a faithful steward, we discover a second audience listening in. The second group of listeners is a pack of religious leaders called the Pharisees. Luke 16:14 notes, "The Pharisees, who were lovers of money, heard all these things, and they ridiculed him." The Pharisees laughed at Jesus. The Pharisees ridiculed Jesus because they loved money. They mocked the Maker of Life's thoughts regarding money because they loved everything about money. They howled at the Son of God, and the root of their bellowing originated from the throne of their hearts straining under the weight of earthly treasure.

This is Jesus we are talking about, and they laughed at Him. Their love of money led them to cackle at the King of Kings. Paul describes the second member of the Godhead, the Son of God, in this way: "He is the image of the invisible God, the first born of all creation. For by him all things were created, in heaven and on earth, visible and invisible, whether thrones or dominions or rulers or authorities—all things were created through him and for him. And he is before all things, and in him all things hold together. And he is the head of the body, the church. He is the beginning, the firstborn from the dead, that in everything he might be preeminent. For in him all the fullness of God was pleased to dwell, and through him to reconcile to himself all things, whether on earth or in heaven, making peace by the blood of his cross" (Col. 3:15-20).

Now, in light of that description, consider the weight of the Pharisees' actions. They ridiculed the image of God in the flesh. They mocked the one who created thrones, dominions, rulers, and authorities. They laughed at the one by whom all things were created; they jeered at the for whom all things were created. They sneered at the one who is before all things, and in whom all things hold together. They cackled at the one who is head of the body, the church. They howled at the one in whom the fullness of God was pleased to dwell. They burst out in laughter at the one through whom God would reconcile to Himself all things through His blood shed on a cross. That person, Jesus Christ—they laughed at Him because they loved money. They loved money more than their maker. They ridiculed the treasure of heaven because they worshipped the treasure of earth.

The third characteristic of a steward is that a steward loves heaven more than treasure while a squanderer loves treasure more than heaven (Luke 16:14). Do you remember the rich young ruler? That guy had it all. Cash, time on his side, power, and prestige. He was sexy, wealthy, and healthy. He was powerful and prestigious. He had the college education, was a successful entrepreneur, and seemed to lack for nothing. However, he was lacking one thing. He came up to Jesus in Luke 18 with these words: "What must I do to inherit eternal life?"

The Son of God thought to Himself and responded by saying, "You know the commandments," insinuating that the man was to obey all of them.

Presumptuousness abounded as the young celebrity quickly dismissed the prescription. "Yes, I have already kept all of those since I was a boy."

Jesus stopped, stared, and then, looking into the man's soul, said, "One thing you still lack. Go, sell all that you have and distribute it to the poor. When you do this, you will have treasure in heaven, and then come follow me." So what happened next? The Bible says the man was sad—very sad. The reason for his sadness was his wealth. He loved the treasure of earth too much to forego it and receive the treasure of heaven. He loved his wealth more than he loved God. Jesus pointed out the idol in his heart, and the man refused to serve only one master in God. Instead, he chose the master he was all too familiar with: money. He squandered his eternal reward of following Jesus because he loved his earthly treasure too much. He forsook a mansion in heaven to dwell in his mansion on earth.

God desires for you to steward His money. He is the land-owner; we are the steward. The psalmist sings, "The earth is the Lord's, and the fullness thereof, the world and those who dwell therein" (Psalm 24:1). It all belongs to God. It all belongs to Jesus, our King. God desires for us to steward this world and to steward our resources. It is not the will of our Creator and Father to find us squandering that which is given to us to manage, steward, and account for. Stewards are faithful for the future; squanderers are destructive to their destiny. Stewards serve only one master; squanderers serve many. Stewards treasure heaven over earth; squanderers treasure earth over heaven. You cannot serve two masters. One leads to treasure in heaven; the other leads to pain and a faithless life. Who will you choose to be? It's an important question, for we will all give an account for our lives one day.

Talk About It

1. Derek shared how his parents influenced him at a young age regarding how to view his finances. How have your parents influenced you regarding how you handle money?
2. What is a great truth (or life lesson) regarding money that has shaped how you think about the subject?
3. We are called to use our money to share the gospel, and so make friendships that will carry on into heaven. How are you using your money to share the gospel or support the gospel?
4. A squanderer is destructive to his destiny. How can we easily squander our finances and ruin our future?
5. A squanderer seeks to serve two masters, God and money. What are the dangers of attempting this service strategy regarding money?
6. What caused the Pharisees to laugh at Jesus, and what caused the rich young ruler to walk away from following Jesus?

Do It

1. Identify one person who stewards their finances in a godly manner. Approach them this week and schedule a time to meet and ask for advice concerning how to begin stewarding your money well for the kingdom of God
2. Make a commitment to give a monthly portion of your income to God. Pray and consider both the amount and recipient of this financial gift.

NOTES

1. Kristin Salaky, "34 People Reveal Their Biggest First Date Horror Stories – Prepare to Cringe," Business Insider, October 17, 2018, https://www.independent.co.uk/life-style/34-people-reveal-their-biggest-first-date-horror-stories-a7918516.html.

2. Jason Chein, et al., "Peers increase adolescent risk taking by enhancing activity in the brain's reward circuitry," *Developmental Science* vol. 14,2 (2011): F1-10. doi:10.1111/j.1467-7687.2010.01035.x.

3. Love Worth Finding with Adrian Rogers, "Making Friends Forever," March 27, 2015, accessed October 4, 2019, https://www.lwf.org/sermon-outlines/making-friends-forever.

4. Love Worth Finding with Adrian Rogers, "Making Friends Forever," March 27, 2015, accessed October 4, 2019, https://www.lwf.org/sermon-outlines/making-friends-forever.

5. Howard Dayton, Your Money Counts: The Biblical Guide to Earning, Spending, Saving, Investing, Giving, and Getting Out of Debt (Carol Stream, IL: Tyndale House Publishers, 2011), 5.

6. Dayton, Your Money Counts, 5.

ABOUT THE AUTHOR

Derek A. Nicksich is a Christian, pastor, author, husband and father. His greatest accomplishment is convincing his beautiful wife to say, "I do." He is the proud father of Nora Allyn, Maverick Abel, and Miles Alistair.

He currently serves and worships as a student minister at Cool Spring Baptist Church in Mechanicsville, VA. He recently authored his first book, **The LILOE Devotional: A Thirty Day Journey of Living in Light of Eternity**, available on Amazon.

Connect with the author: dereknicksich.wordpress.com

ALSO AVAILABLE BY DEREK A. NICKSICH

What matters most in life?

Health, wealth, and happiness will never bring ultimate contentment. In fact, they don't even answer the question about priorities in life. What matters most in life is God. From the creator of the universe flows every good gift.

The purpose of The LILOE Devotional (pronounced LEE-LOW) is to provide thirty days of biblical truth, insight, and inspiration about what really matters in life. Living in Light of Eternity is the call of every Christian. Reasonably priced, and available in both paperback and kindle editions, this book is filled with scripture verses, devotional insights, guided prayer, and practical application suggestions to immediately translate your talk of eternity today into a walk of eternity tomorrow.

Available for purchase on Amazon.

Printed in the United States
By Bookmasters